Praise for **Invitation to Love** by Moriah

During this very disruptive time in our world's history, *Invitation To Love* has arrived "right on time." It's clarity in the midst of chaos. *Invitation To Love* is the calm, clear, yet ever so softly spoken voice we often hear from within ourselves. We feel Its truth, sadly though, we often dismiss it as unheard. At its core, is the message of Love toward ourselves, for one another, and for our Source of All That Is. And, as I took the inner journey into an *Invitation To Love*, I developed a deeper Love [and trust] for this special voice that resides within my Self, *this* same voice within each of us. It was as if *my* inner voice was speaking to me the words my heart already has known for lifetimes. I found *Invitation To Love* as the world's universal guidance system for each of us to return to [the Source] of Love necessary to connect to the purpose of our existence, the evolution of our soul, the unity of our worlds.

The message in an *Invitation To Love* felt familiar to me and I believe you will have a similar experience.

Glenn E. Kakely is author of *Your Power to Create You:*
Discover Your Inner Source of Abundance
Board Certified Hypnotist, Reiki Master,
Natural Wellness Educator-Consultant,
New York.

Moriah is a highly accomplished yet humble Spiritual Master. As I went through her beautiful book, Invitation to Love, the lines seemed to be a Conversation with God...A great teacher is one who knows what the student seeks. The great doctor is one who knows where the pain of the patient resides. A great author is one who knows what the reader needs. However, there is no great teacher, doctor or author who can teach, treat or resolve every issue on this earth. I accurately know now, why *'Invitation to Love'* by Moriah is indeed a 'Sacred Text'.

I am happy to find something fool-proof and handy as an optimum relief for any pain-body, a Midas touch for any disillusioned mind, and a magical healing for any tormented soul.

Asit Ghosh is an accomplished Inspirational Speaker,
Trainer, Behavioral Specialist, Life Coach,
Management Consultant and Author
India.

I was astounded by how many of the words from this sacred text were a reflection of my own journey. *Invitation to Love* offers the reader much truth and wisdom. It is a spiritual road map to our best and highest selves.

Joe Hazen, INHC, is an Integrative
Nutrition Health Coach,
New York.

"What is Love?" has been the question posed by humans since the beginning of time. In her book, Moriah has given us the answer from those closest to its source..Angelic beings who call themselves the Teachers of Love. Rarely, if ever, have sacred texts for our times been channeled as they have been in this amazing book, Invitation to Love. As one reads, one is reminded that these are the voices of angelic beings speaking to us, and not merely another book about Love. It is indeed an invitation to love emanating from the mind and heart of God, the Source of all to whom we shall all return. That return to Home, as these Teachers of Love refer to it, now has a guidebook in Invitation to Love. These sacred channeled texts are for our Age, for our journey back to Source in these troubled, turbulent times. This invitation to love is not extended to only us on Planet Earth, but to beings throughout the vast Universe. The Teachers of Love have knowledge of other-worldly entities, and seek to have them join with us on our journey back Home to Source from which we all have come.

Diane Hale Smith, Theologian,
Educator, Musician, Photographer;
Co-Founder of Centro Civico
Amsterdam, NY.

Invitation to Love is an insightful guide to a more fulfilling, rewarding life, with God's Love and our Love for each other at the center of our being.

Ruby Dean Collins is author of Mountain Treasures,
West Virginia.

For those who ponder the meaning of life and where things are headed for us individually, as a society, and as a planet, *Invitation To Love* will address it in a richly meaningful, yet simple enough way. This is a book which can be read over and over, and will speak to you at different levels as you move along your path. It brought peace to me in an area of life that I struggled with for many years, simply by showing me that we will all get there. We are helped along, as we help others along, creating a chain of love and connection that moves our planet towards its higher good. Arriving at one's own commitment to a Life of Love will be incredibly rewarding, more so than any other distraction or pleasure of life.

Lisa Nelson, HTCP, is an Author, Musician and
Healing Touch Practitioner
New Jersey.

Spiritual Master Moriah shares pure, genuine wisdom in *Invitation to Love*. This guide to everything, from true, right relationships to opportunities for connection and joining, is insightful and THE way forward for the future.

Janet Tanguay is a Creativity Coach
and owner of Art n Soul, Inc
New York.

Invitation to Love

from the
Teachers of Love
through a
Messenger named Moriah

Moriah is the spiritual name the Teachers of Love have given to Sue Kidd Shipe-Hart, PhD, who has bridged this text to the physical realm.

Copyright 2016 All rights reserved.
ISBN: 0970946120 ISBN-13: 978-0970946126
International Institute For Human Empowerment, Inc.

The Teachers of Love are giving The New Message of Love to guide Humanity through the evolution that is occurring. <u>Invitation to Love</u> is part of this Message.

<u>Invitation to Love</u> is given here as it was received, with minimal editing in order to maintain its authenticity.

> "We humans do not understand Divine Mystery. We receive. We acknowledge the Source. We share in order to move others forward. It is so ordained."
>
> — Moriah

For more information on **The New Message of Love**, go to www.newworldempowerment.org

The beauty and greatness of love is without equal.

It is timeless.

It is everlasting.

It will be with us through eternity.

And so it is.

                                                Moriah

Forward

"Make me a channel of Your peace, that where there is hatred, I might sow love." This powerful prayer by St. Francis of Assisi was on my lips and in my heart as I prepared for, received, and now make public, this sacred text. None of it could have happened without life preparation: those influences that moved my spiritual evolution through many phases.

How does one begin to name and express gratitude to all those who have taught, brought lessons, and supported one's journey through life? I am sure to be remiss of naming all, but some stand out as beacons along the way. Hallie "Mom" Conrad, my maternal grandmother, was my first and most prominent spiritual teacher. Her simple and profound faith was part of all of her daily life. Spending time with her, as I was growing up in a small town in West Virginia, brought to me a perspective of living faith that I have seldom witnessed. God to her was love, and she gave her family love without condition.

In my early years, the Sutton Baptist Church was the center of my social life and spiritual growth. Its lack of hierarchy contributed to my acceptance of prayer as direct access, and an easy transition to receiving. As I moved into college and beyond, I spent time in the Episcopal, Methodist, Unitarian and Unity Churches. Each provided something more, but not enough. It is said that when the student is ready, the teacher appears, and spiritual teachers came at just the right time to guide me. Ram Dass and Dr. Wayne Dyer challenged my thinking. Marshall Vian Summers initiated me into experience. I began to publish anonymously as Moriah, and also under my given name. Joy Adler supported me as I prepared to take the role of Moriah publicly.

Simultaneously, other pioneers who risked their lives and careers in search of truth, came into my life. Dr. John Mack, Budd Hopkins, Peter Robbins, Larry Warren, Richard Dolan, and Audrey Hewins are only a few. Each one brought light to existential areas of thinking that most people choose not to see. Richard Dolan and Bryce Zabel invited us to consider the fate of our world when our notion of reality becomes challenged. All of our institutions will need to expand in order to accept and integrate this greater reality in the New World. Those institutions that are unable will become irrelevant. The process has already begun.

I want to give special thanks to those who support me personally. My adult children and their families are my world. They allow me to grow and explore the unknown, with the knowledge that they are my steadfast foundation. Unending thanks go to my husband Brian Hart, who never fails to support me with his amazing capacity for love, and yet to be discovered, possibilities.

Thank you to Lisa Nelson, my editor, who understood from the beginning the need to maintain the authenticity of The Teachers of Love, so that you, the reader, could benefit from each precious word.

A heartfelt thank you to my talented daughter Erica Shipe Dodd who designed the book cover after I described for her a vision I was given of a rose arising from the ground. The vision occurred at the time I was receiving the beautiful description of life unfolding like the opening of a rose. The poignant design captures the essence of receiving from beyond.

"Make me a channel of Your peace..." that this sacred text may help us all to expand our capacity to love, including all that we are yet unable to fathom. May we gently grow together. May Invitation to Love draw you into unprecedented spiritual growth. And may we, together, make this Universe we share a better place for all.

A Note to the Reader

Moriah is the spiritual name of Sue Kidd Shipe-Hart, Ph.D. At an early age, she longed for God, and found Spirit to be her companion through adversity. Always feeling that she had a master destiny not yet revealed to her, she looked for signs that she was to abandon a more traditional career in education, for a new career in higher spiritual education. This revelation came to her in 1990, and in early 1991 she received *Invitation to Love*.

Invitation to Love is now being shared publicly. May you treat it with the dignity and respect it deserves, for you are about to read Sacred Text.

Words such as love and peace are capitalized when they refer to the Divine. Disciple of Love is capitalized when it is used as a title that denotes a high level of life commitment of the one on the spiritual path.

Introduction

Invitation to Love was received by Moriah in 1991. It was given over a period of approximately five months, one chapter at a sitting. Now, 25 years later, it is being made public. Its message is relevant to our time as we increasingly move forward as a global community through communication and technology, exponentially expanding our knowledge of our planet and our universe, continuously challenging notions of "reality" and our scientific paradigm–and literally, reaching for the stars. We are increasing our awareness of ourselves internally and externally as we progress.

At such an important juncture in human evolution, while many people still view human life as the only life in the Universe, an intervention called "The New Message of Love" is offering to us a broader and higher perspective of reality. We are given a vision of our evolving earth and the challenges the human race will face. We are helped to understand that while we struggle with accepting human diversity, we will be given a greater challenge as we expand into a universal community. What we learn here may amaze and challenge us, but we are also given a way to adapt to this change. Invitation to Love is one part of a broader message, The New Message of Love, being given to us through Moriah by the highest level of spiritual entities known as Angels, or Teachers. Their messages will continue to be received and added to the writings that form the basis for New World Empowerment Ministries. More information can be found at www.newworldempowerment.org.

If at first your mind is rejecting of this new information, simply read, and then let it be. Everywhere our paradigms are shifting. What was once believed impossible is now possible. What was once accepted as the norm is now outdated, even obsolete. Reflect on the change you have witnessed during your lifetime, and you may find little today that is even remotely reminiscent of the lives of your parents and grandparents.

The next great step in spiritual evolution will be based less on faith in another's story, and more on personal experience. This is not to challenge, but to build upon existing religious and spiritual beliefs. We are opening to new experience, and as we do, our lives become more relevant. Here we are given a way to achieve and maintain stability while our world shifts. Old ways of thinking, living, believing, moving about, and even viewing ourselves within this ever-expanding universe are changing. What we believe, the institutions we've trusted, and our view of life purpose, are all shifting as well. We search for the meaning of our existence and wonder why we are here.

These age-old questions find new meaning in spiritual experience if we are open to it. However, we cannot yet imagine the beauty, life, purpose, and fulfillment this contains.

You have come here for more. What you long for is here. What you need is here. What the human race needs for its successful evolution is here. Open your heart to receive the Invitation to Love.

Invitation to Love

A Gift from the Teachers of Love to Humanity

The Invitation

Devotion to God is the highest order of Love. Love has many levels and manifestations. Your people use love when they mean fantasy of romance, acceptance, caring. Yet these levels of love do not generally require surrender and sacrifice.

Higher levels of Love may require more of one's self to be given. In romance, one is seeking self-satisfaction and self-aggrandizement. In other words, one's ego is generally boosted as one is placed upon a pedestal and admired, and one might find this quite satisfying until life experiences create a reality that does not allow for this to continue. Caring may be made manifest in many ways and is most essential to the proper nourishment of all people. Caring is the emotional environment that promotes growth. Yet, Love, as it is a manifestation of God, may require that all that one has be given.

When one loves in this manner, one seeks the highest good. One chooses actions based upon understanding from one's higher self. This view is from a different perspective than the perspective that celebrates romance. In other words, relationship based upon the highest good emanating from one's higher self will be that which is manifest by higher purpose.

Love that devotes all of self to God is the highest order of love, yet it must be emanating from one's higher self. In other words, it is sometimes seen in your world that there are those who proclaim to love God, to seek followers, yet their actions are for their own aggrandizement. When one gives oneself to God, there are no accolades. There is only fulfillment. That fulfillment is unity with the Godhead. This unity with the Godhead is what joins all within the universe. Thus, all joining is becoming one with God.

The spiral of Love moves through many levels. One must go through many incarnations to reach the level of devotion to God. Thus, one must not look out upon the world and judge the world, but recognize that all are joining. All are in process. All are returning. One must not feel sad for another who cannot join, but see that they are on a path of learning so that they may be able to contribute. Many incarnations must be provided for this learning to occur, and one must also be able to see beyond the glitter of the world.

One comes to devotion to God through disillusionment. Therefore, as long as one is somewhat satisfied by the world's offerings, one will not come into the desire to devote one's life in service to one's higher purpose, to God. Therefore, one can only come to God through disillusionment. It is when one has tried to find fulfillment in the many areas available within your world that one becomes resigned or disillusioned. One may remain in disillusionment or may use this disillusionment as a catalyst to propel them into a newer life. This new life is a life devoted to one's calling in the world. Therefore, it is only through the pain of disillusionment that one may be reclaimed.

All who join are being reclaimed, as all were once joined. Incarnations are the separation of one from all others. It is this decision to incarnate, to learn and contribute, that creates separation, and it is the decision to accept the Invitation to Love that causes one to return. Therefore, in each incarnation one is given the opportunity to join. Most will go through many incarnations, and upon joining, will move forward into the next level. A few will be given the choice to return upon having accomplished joining. They will bring a Message incarnate. The Message will be of God.

Those who return incarnate will need support by those preparing to join, and they will move together to the next level upon completion of their assignment. Therefore, the chain is unbroken as those from Beyond give the Message to those who choose to return, who offer the Invitation to all others to join. Those who become incarnate out of a decision to return as Messengers must carry a heavy responsibility alone. Yet they are never truly alone. The memory of Home must be reclaimed as one loses all memory upon entering the earthplane. Your people are without memory of Home. They must reclaim their memory. They must join in order to return. Therefore, this Message is the Invitation to Love, to join, and to return.

You are invited. None may be excluded. All are encouraged to join. Let your life be given in devotion to God that God might work through you and thus bless and reclaim your world. This is most essential as your world continues in its evolution, as this evolution will be the bringing together of beings of many worlds. This is already occurring. You must turn away from the glitter of the world and make a true choice, the choice to fulfill your purpose and calling in the world that you might move forward and that the Universe might become One. Thus all are joining. All are returning. All will eventually be One.

Chapter One

The Word of God is made manifest among you. It is the reclamation of intuition that will bring all to peace and love. It is God's will that your planet reclaim intuition that all might return Home. Honor those who are reclaiming throughout your Universe. It is to be desired that all shall follow.

Do not allow those desires of your personal self to draw you away, as they are only vapors that disappear in light of day. They sparkle, they glitter, they draw you like an oasis draws a thirsty man, yet only that which is of God shall be reclaimed. Therefore, it is your people, your community, that is to be the leadership of your planet. They will assist in bringing forth peace and love. It is only when your desire nature is true that others will recognize your devotion and follow. Therefore, it is not to first draw upon others, it is to first purify yourselves. Take this word to all who will truly commit their lives to their spiritual purpose. It is in the commitment and bringing forth one's purpose that others are drawn.

One must move forward alone, willingly acknowledging that God is all one needs. It is when one can let go of oneself, that one draws what is needed to them. Therefore, let your lives be unburdened. Let your souls be purified. Let your desire be for God. Speak to no one of your purpose, for your purpose will speak to all.

Do not allow that which would be unrequited take you away from all that is of eternity. Speak of love and peace. Live love and peace, that love and peace may speak to the world. It is

God's plan that all should follow; therefore, move forward that others may see God's peace and love and be reclaimed.

The Love of God is deeper, stronger, more enduring, and completely fulfilling. It will be the manna for your soul. Therefore, from this date forward, let nothing take you away from that for which you have been anointed.

Speak only of God's love, God's peace, that they may abide with you and through you. Allow all who would to follow and bring forth all that is of God. Your light must now begin to truly shine, that the world might see and yield.

God is Love. God is Peace. God is Intuition. God is Trinity. One experiences God in the realms of intuition, love and peace. Let the Trinity be the redemption of your planet.

Love is the fulfillment of the heart's greatest desire. It is the reclaiming of the world to God. Love is the vehicle that transports one to that place where all longing is fulfilled. Love provides the answers to all of life's questions. It takes away doubt. It heals wounds. It guides the lost. It promotes the bringing of your planet to its ultimate conclusion. The ultimate conclusion is the returning of all to God. Therefore, it is the bringing forth of Love that will provide your planet the necessary means to return Home.

You are beginning that total Love experience. It is the desire to give all of oneself to God. It is the desire to hold back nothing. It is magnetic. It is that which the more one experiences, the more one desires to give. Therefore, once one begins to accept Love, one surrenders personal power and gains the power of the Godseed. As you move forward in Love, as you truly allow yourselves to become channels of Love, you will lose yourselves more and more completely until all has been released.

As you move forward to make this eternal commitment, you are letting go of all that you have known to gain all that you truly long for. The world does not define that longing and seeks to fill it with those things that are only temporary. There is much sadness, much pain, much suffering within your planet. This is created by looking in the wrong places to find one's true fulfillment. It is by stepping forward that one can truly move into the Light and allow all else to fall away that one might become one with One. It is as you move into the Light that you return Home. You accept Home and bring Home into your world, but you are already Home.

As you move forward in the world, your experiences will change because you have changed within yourself. You will begin to see differently, to hear differently, to experience the world as a place where healing can come through you. Therefore, the healing power of Love will go out into the world and touch all pain and suffering.

The presence of those who are in this Light, who are channels of Love, is both disruptive and healing. Therefore, one must be prepared to witness what is occurring to realize that the presence of Love is at work, and to allow Love to do what It must to allow change to occur.

Love is power. It enters and does not leave. It ignites without consuming. It propels one so that one no longer wishes to control in the way one once did. It is by allowing yourself to release control, to become unburdened, that you become channels for Love. Let your prayers be that you might relinquish all. Let nothing keep you from the Love of God. Be willing to step forward alone, that others might join you, for it is in the willingness to be alone that one is never alone. One gains when one gives up. One moves forward when one stops running, when one allows Love to imbue their lives and move them in Love's direction.

Love knows nothing but Love. It cannot recognize what it does not already know. Therefore, Its presence will be most challenging. When one is a channel for Love, one must be able to move about, knowing that disturbances will always occur. One will make others feel uneasy, doubt themselves, fear; and the fear will sometimes cause others to strike out. Therefore, one must be most cautious as the power of their presence can create difficulties they might not otherwise be aware of. It is important that as you move forward, you be aware of others' reactions to you. You must be most discerning for your own protection, aware that another's response may be harsh or one of aggression. Yet Love will provide the healing that is required. It will provide the acknowledgement of all that needs to change. It will not allow things to remain as they are.

As you move forward into this light, you will become purified. You will find yourselves being transformed so that you cannot return to your former self. The commitment you are about to make is your decision to follow God. God is Love. God is Peace. God is Intuition. God is Trinity. The world is in need of these mighty words so that it might return. Therefore, move forward and allow nothing to take you away from fulfilling your purpose.

Meditate on Love, that Love might fill you, might consume you, might propel you, might move eternally through you, to bless your world.

Be at peace and all else will follow.

Love is the devotion of one's heart to its Source. Love brings together all who would join. It will be the redemption of the Universe.

Love asks not what can be done for It, but what one can do. It is when one loves that one allows oneself to be magnetically drawn to the Source of all being.

Love enhances all that is of its own. It saves the world from its own destruction. It is when those who are drawn join together that Love moves forward in the world. It is the moving forward that unifies, that allows the Universe to become One.

Love melds separateness into one eternal being. It draws together positive force and repels all negative energy. That is why one must begin with self-love. When one loves oneself, one can be the positive energy that draws, that joins, that creates, that magnifies all that has preceded.

As the joining occurs, it is like a ball of energy. The ball becomes larger, brighter, more magnetic. It draws more toward it. That is why, as you develop self-love, as you join in small groups, these similar groups come together and begin that positive energy field that will draw all back to the Source.

Love is joining. It is expressed in relationship. That is why it is most essential that when you join, you join another positive force. It is when these two forces come together, they create more than what was once separate. They are more than double. Therefore, the sum is far greater than the parts.

You want peace in your world, yet peace comes from joining. Peace is the product of that which is joined. When you join with others, you will create peace in that part of your world. Therefore, it is important to continue these joinings. These joinings are happening at both levels of your universe. They are happening among people, and they will happen in the greater universe. It is as these different levels come together, all are drawn upon.

When you are a channel for Love and Peace, you are God's magnet. You are drawn to join with that which is positive. This positive energy is at the level of the higher self, yet it is the personal self that can be most destructive. Therefore, though one sees through the eye of Love, and sees another's higher self, one must be most discerning that one does not join with the negativity of the personal self. One therefore must have double vision. One must be able to see the beauty of the higher self, yet one must be able to look without judgment, without preference, without fear, at the manifestation of the personal self.

One can only join when the energy from the personal self is positive. Therefore it is important to send out your energy to attract all that are positive. It is important to send Love and Peace to those who are not yet ready to join. They will join in time, so do not become distraught about them, as it is not yet their time for joining. It is this positive energy that comes through those who are channels for Peace and Love that must attract other positive energy.

Love joins positive energy into a magnificent, positive force. This positive force continues to grow. As it multiplies, it brings Peace in the hearts of those who are redeemed. Therefore, Love and Peace are truly One. As these mighty works are taken into the world, they will each manifest. They will each grow. They will join and bring together all who will respond.

The Love of God captures, sanctifies, all that It joins. It purifies all that is Its own. Once purified, Love gives of Itself and becomes a dynamic force. Its magnetic field becomes stronger as it grows.

Love does not know negativity. That is why all negativity, all that is not aligned with Love, falls away. This is the process of purification. This purification makes one acceptable as the offering, as the light, as the energy of God.

This energy goes through one and into the world without one's effort. One's effort is directed at maintaining that purity, of that single-mindedness that one belongs only to God. Therefore, the purification process is never complete until one is Home, yet as one draws closer to Home, one's desire becomes greater, one has less resistance, and one knows that Home is what one desires most of all.

Therefore, let your prayers be that you may be sanctified, that you may be purified, that you may release all that would separate you from this holiness, and that you might forever be channels of Love and Peace.

The world is not accepting. The world fights that which it does not understand. The world is like a frightened child. It becomes threatened and retaliates at all that does not appear to belong. Therefore, those who become channels of Peace and Love must be discerning. They must always be aware of the power that emanates from them. This is not their power. This is not personal power. This is the power of God.

The channel for Love and Peace cannot control the power, cannot control the response to the power. They can only control their own behavior. They must be with Intuition in making all choices. They must know with whom to share, and with whom they may not.

The Love of God satisfies, fulfills, and brings one to everlasting peace. One finds peace as one allows oneself to be purified.

Let your lives be pure, be open, be receptive. Be channels for Love and Peace, that the world might be redeemed, that all might return to the Source.

Love is the heart's full bloom. It is what the heart most longs for. As one grows in the understanding of love, one feels like a bud that is opening, that is bringing forth its full fragrance into the world. As the bud grows and develops, it is at first very tight. It is not open. Yet the internal growth that is continuing within its outer shell causes it to at some point burst that outer shell. As it opens, it begins to emit its fragrance. It begins to receive stimuli from the rest of the world. Its petals are exposed. It is more at the mercy of the elements. It needs to be able to receive the light, the water, the nutrients of the soil, in order to continue to grow.

You are like the bud. As you develop your training, knowing that you have desire for love, but are not yet exposed, you become like a bud that grows until it finally bursts its outer shell. During that internal growth period, you are at first most disillusioned. You are tiny, you are compact; the gentle love of the world cannot reach you through your shell. It is only as this disillusionment becomes most intense that you begin to filter in ideas, information, relationships that cause you to begin to grow. As these new ideas begin to take hold, you are growing and growing until this outer shell bursts and you are ready for experience. Once you have reached the stage where you can begin to experience the love of God, and to recognize it as experience, you are also most vulnerable to strong winds, to heavy rain, to snow and hail, to drought, to lack of nutrients, to lack of those things that would allow you to continue to grow.

Therefore, like the bud which has just burst, you must surround yourself with those who will support your growth, who will love you unconditionally. You must let go of those things in your life that no longer nurture your new discoveries, that will not allow you to move forward. It is this unburdening that is a somewhat difficult part of growth. Yet as those petals reach forward into the sun, they cannot return to the casing that once covered them, that once kept them from all they could experience. That is why, as you move forward into spiritual experience, you cannot return to the bud you once were. The bud is tight. It is closed. It is impenetrable. It is so small, so hard, so closed that it will wither if not nourished. The person on the spiritual path is like the bud growing until it bursts, and then having experience with those things that it needs to be nurtured, and to develop further. If it does not receive these nutrients, it cannot go forward.

Every decision in life now becomes most important in supporting the one who is opening to God's love. Every decision must be made in light of its impact on one's spiritual experience. The relationships one develops, the vibrations one experiences, the interpretation one gives, are all most important. As one begins to have spiritual experience, one begins simultaneously to encounter many who will deny the experience. They are most afraid of disillusionment. They will choose to interpret these events in light of their own experience. If they are of important position in society, they are given much credibility. Their words are given much weight. Therefore, while the criticism of some does not necessarily contain a threat to the one on the spiritual path, the writings and thoughts expressed by those held in high esteem can pose a severe threat because of their personal power. Therefore one must realize on the spiritual path, one is responsible for one's own interpretation of events.

It is important to be surrounded by those who have interpretations of events that are realistic, that are honest, yet are seeking higher purpose. It is important that they be discerning, yet that they not have their vision limited by current and old ways of thinking. They must be open, they must be able to realize that it is not possible to interpret these events within your current systems. Your science, mathematics, literature cannot explain that which the person on the spiritual path may experience. Therefore it is important to be able to trust one's intuition, as one must consult one's intuition to interpret the experience.

Spiritual work is like being on the cutting edge, as one is open to new realms of understanding. One does not have a current system in place for one to recognize and understand these events. One's only way of filtering and testing these events is with their own intuition. That is why the person on the spiritual path must be most grounded, and must have spiritual understanding and intuition available to assist their interpretation. Without this, people have had most amazing experiences, but have been left afraid and unable to function effectively in the world.

As you move forward in the experience of God's love, it is important to have a foundation for interpreting experience. Therefore, one must cultivate one's intuition in conjunction with experience to be able to sustain this work. Without the cultivation of intuition, one is like a flower that opens to the elements and is pushed back. It is as if intuition were the firm roots under the soil that cannot be seen, that cannot be felt, yet it is the recipient of the nutrients. It selects the nutrients needed and filters these nutrients into ways that they will be used for the support and growth of the new blossom.

As you develop in God's love, your roots must become most strong. They must be well developed under the soil. They must provide the support system for all new growth and experience. Therefore, your ability to assimilate spiritual experience is directly proportional to your ability to be with intuition.

One on a spiritual path must have deep desire. It is like the desire of the blossom for the sun. Your desire for your Source is like the desire of the blossom to face the sun. If it is denied sun, it will not flourish. It will turn in the direction of the sun. It will stretch its stems, its leaves, in that direction also. It will reach, as nothing else can nourish it. If it is denied the sun altogether, it will die.

If you, as one on a spiritual path, are denied your Source, you will not be able to continue. Therefore you must seek, you must desire, you must make time for receiving the nourishment of God. The blossom must spend time daily in the presence of the sun. You must also spend time daily in the presence of your Source to receive the nutrients you need for continued growth. This is why, at any time, you can lose your opportunity to blossom by being denied your Source and by failing to cultivate intuition within.

As you move into this light of Source, like the blossom that leans toward the sun, you will become most beautiful. You are full of promise like the bud, yet you must be able to develop, to lose your shell, and to desire and seek the nutrients you need in order for the promise to be fulfilled. The promise of the bud is that it will fully blossom, become totally open, and give all of its fragrance to the world. You are designed to open, to give all that has been prepared, into the world.

Love is the final review of the opportunities and choices one receives within one's life span. Love is the final opportunity to become that for which one has been designed. It is when one enters into the earth life that one comes prepared to reveal one's purpose to the world. One's purpose has already been determined. This purpose was agreed upon before one came into the earthplane. It was arranged to meet the requirements of acquiring the next step in one's own evolution. This evolutionary process is ongoing until one returns to one's Source. It is like a magnificent ladder. Each rung represents a step of accomplishment, the acquisition of learning and the demonstration of that learning in the form of contribution. The world is a place much in need of the contribution of each person. There will be peace when each person contributes that which he has brought with him into the world to contribute. Therefore, as each discovers his purpose, as each contributes that purpose to the world, the world is coming closer to that state of oneness called peace.

Peace is the unity of all that has been created. It is more than the absence of war. It is more than the receiving all of one's desires for personal acquisition. It is the complete unification of all that God has created. Therefore, peace begins internally with one's own self-love, and continues to encompass all others until there is total acceptance. The world is to be loved unconditionally in its current state. One cannot wait to love. One must accept all that is and contribute to the current state without judgment. When one accepts oneself, another, one's community, the world as it is, one is filled with internal peace and love. That peace and love flows into the world as positive energy. Thus, when one becomes accepting, one simultaneously becomes a channel for peace and love. This will be the redemption of the world.

When all are accepting, when all become channels for peace and love, there will be peace among you. This acceptance is the lack of judgment that says, "I love you just as you are. I see your strengths. I see your weaknesses. Together they combine to bring about this most beautiful person with much to contribute to the world."

One cannot wait until one is without weakness to contribute to the world, as one at this level will always have weakness. Therefore one must accept oneself as one is, realizing that one is uniquely designed to bring forth a purpose. That purpose is not dependent on all strengths. It is dependent upon the combination of specific strengths and specific weaknesses. It is essential as you become more aware that you are designed to bring forth contribution into the world, that you begin to look at your life. You have acquired much that is not relevant to what you are discovering is your purpose.

Your purpose will require your focus. Before you discover your purpose, the whole world is your option. You can pick and choose from a vast array, yet as you become aware of your purpose, your must pare down and choose only those things which are in alignment with your purpose. When one is paring down one's life to prepare for contribution, one may feel pain at giving up those things one has found to be important.

Yet it is this unburdening that brings one into the light and prepares one to be a full contributor. Thus by giving up, one gains all that one is designed to fulfill. One has the opportunity to take that next step on one's evolutionary ladder.

Love is the final redemption of the heart's longing for its Source. At this stage one has conscious awareness of one's desire for God. Through lifetimes one has learned the lessons to be learned, and has assimilated that which was to have been part of that preparation. One has agreed upon the task to be given to the world in order to take another step in the evolution toward Home. As one fulfills the contribution at that step, one takes a giant step in one's own evolution. Yet one does much of this outside the conscious awareness that one is moving Home. One knows that one must, as one feels a sense of urgency, yet it is truly the desire for God that brings one to the fulfillment through contribution.

As one progresses into the fulfillment of one's purpose, one finds increased desire to bring that purpose to fruition. One will feel rejuvenated, full of desire, with more life flowing through them. This life they will experience as energy, as enthusiasm, and it will provide the strength to make the decisions that are in alignment with their own purpose. Therefore, moving up this ladder, moving toward the fulfillment of one's purpose, is like being pulled by a giant magnet. As one moves toward the source of that energy, one is drawn most strongly, and that attraction becomes stronger as one moves forward.

Like the tiny bud that has cracked the outer casing, the petals flow forth freely and quickly. They can no longer be contained. They have desire to give of their beauty, of their essence, to the world. Thus one who is fulfilling one's purpose, who has made commitment to that purpose, suddenly finds their lives quickly unfolding and their desire increasing. They find that they have a need to experience the giving of that which they have brought with them. The stage of preparation, which is love, is like the bud which contains much growth. The next stage, which is that of breaking the casing, cannot occur until the preparation is complete. The preparation may appear incomplete, inadequate, as one nears the fulfillment of one's purpose, as one feels oneself being thrust upon the world. Yet the casing cannot break until the preparation is complete. The flower, when it opens, is a total and complete flower. It is small, yet its petals will peel away independently of one another, causing the appearance of rapid growth.

As your casing is broken, and as you emerge on your spiritual path, you cannot return to the bud. The petals can never close together in the manner that they once were. Your life can never go backward; it must go forward. You must bring your gifts to the world, that your gifts can contribute toward the peace of God.

Love is the magnet that draws you to full contribution and the achievement of peace. Love is the redemption of the planet. It is the magnet that pulls all to the Source of all that has been created. It is this love, this acceptance, that promotes the growth of each individual. Therefore, when one is a channel for Love and Peace, one must be aware that one must be most accepting in order that each person will experience what it means to be loved unconditionally, that their own intuition will be activated.

It is the activation of this intuition that brings them to purpose. Therefore, Love is the link between the activation of intuition, and the peace of God. Love is the catalyst. Love is the activator. Love is not always gentle. Love can be most painful as it brings one toward the truth so that they might move forward with their own purpose. Love is both soothing and disruptive. It soothes, in that it stills the unexplained longing within the heart by moving it forward. Yet it is often preceded by disruption, which causes one to move. Therefore, think not that Love is for soothing one into a state of complacency. It is, rather, the motivator of one toward the fulfillment of one's purpose.

As one begins to bring one's purpose into the world, one becomes a channel for love. This Love can be most disruptive. As one is fulfilling one's purpose, one must always be discerning so that one takes care of oneself. Others will react, yet it is not a reaction to one's personality, it is a reaction to the God presence within. Therefore the one who is on the spiritual path, and who has broken that casing and begun to allow one's purpose to be fulfilled, becomes a most disruptive element in the presence of others. One must be loving and accepting, yet one must be most aware and shield oneself. There are those who will be able to participate, who will be able to encounter the truth of acknowledgement that their lives are for a deeper purpose. Those who make this decision in the presence of Love will move forward to contribute their gifts.

Most will not be able to accept and understand the truth, will move away to protect themselves, and if threatened, will strike out. Therefore, the person on the spiritual path must be most non-threatening, must be assertive and able to move forward, yet must not create those situations for direct confrontation that would endanger one. One must be most with Intuition, so that one can discern the level of confrontation of truth that one may bring forth. Therefore, Love is most disruptive as it brings one into position of encountering the truth within them. This is most painful for many, and one must be ready to love and support another as they deal with this truth. That is why honesty is so important when one is on a spiritual path. One must be able to speak the truth, realizing it will cause disruption and possible hurt and anger.

The magnetic force of God pulls all in the direction of returning to the Source. It is that which will bring peace individually, and to the world. It is a contribution of gifts that gives one internal peace and makes one a channel for Peace and Love. Therefore, as one moves forward on the spiritual path, like the flower that is in blossom, one must give all of oneself in the journey. The journey is most glorious and brings people forward to the heart's desire. Ask that God propel you forward on your journey, filling you with lifeforce that keeps your path straight and brings you to the peace that surpasses understanding.

Love is the basis for all relationship. It is the tie that binds one to another. Love brings forward in each that which is best. It promotes the growth of the other. It provides the strength and the support to allow for the other's total growth. Therefore, when one is in true relationship with another one feels most supported; one feels most bound; one desires to give forth love and support. When these qualities are not present in relationship, the relationship is not truly supported by love.

There are many other connections that can bring about relationship, but they are not of the kind that foster true relationship in the world. As one looks at one's relationships, one needs to have criteria for deciding if those relationships support their growth as an individual, toward becoming all that they are to become to fulfill their purpose in the world. One must look to this criteria to determine whether one is supporting oneself in a way that will allow them to bring their lives to this point of fruition.

In determining whether those relationships are supportive, one is not to be judgmental, one is not to desire to hurt another, yet one must be most objective. One must look at the relationship and ask, "Does this relationship support that which I am to do in the world?" If one's life is dedicated to a higher purpose, to a sense of mission, one will have much energy and enthusiasm toward bringing forth that goal into the world. When one is moving toward that goal, one's being is filled with joy, with excitement, with enthusiasm. When one allows other things to clutter that path, one becomes most frustrated and loses sight of one's goal if the clutter is not cleared away. Therefore, one must look as to whether one is feeling enthusiastic, one is feeling excited, one is feeling joyful, to determine if one is clearly focused on their goal. If one does not have these feelings, one should look inward and say, "What are those things, those relationships that are not in support of my reaching this goal?" This is not to look at others and say, "You are the reason I cannot reach my goal. You are hindering me." But rather, "The things that I need to support me are not present here, and I must find that support in order to be able to fulfill my purpose."

When one has a sense of purpose, one also has a sense of the enormity of this purpose. It is not for oneself that one gives, but one gives that the world might be enriched. Therefore this giving is essential for the betterment of the world. It is not that one should feel better than, inflated over, others, but that one is contributing that which they have the capability to contribute so that the world might be a better place for all to experience and grow. Therefore, as one looks at one's relationships, one must question first what it is one needs. "Do I feel supported? Do I feel that this person with whom I am in relationship truly understands what it is that I am doing, that I must do, and would be able to contribute toward that goal?"

It is not enough that another does not hinder us; it is that the goal can be supported mutually. That is, that both can contribute toward the same goal. This must be a mutual goal in which the two people have different roles to play. One will often be the one who is in the world. This person encounters the people with whom they must participate in order to bring this goal to accomplishment. The other is a more supportive role, going into the world as indicated. Their purpose is often to be the emotional support, the one who takes care of the details, the one who organizes, and the one who soothes the other when the world is not accepting. Both roles are equally important, yet one is more highly visible.

As we look at our relationships we must determine if those relationships indeed support what we believe to be our goal or higher purpose in life. Lack of resistance alone is not enough to say one is being supported, as the fact that another merely does not interfere is not true support. When one looks at relationships, however, and sees interference, one knows that one must relinquish that relationship as that relationship will take them away from the goal and the sense of fulfillment in their lives. If one is a teacher, loves one's students, and desires to contribute to their highest good, one is enthusiastic about this position and needs to be with another who is supportive of that goal. If one is not being supported, one must ask honestly for that support. One must ask the other if they are capable of giving that support. The other must make that determination. Then one must also look at those things that are inhibiting, and ask the other to release or stop those things. If the other cannot accept this, cannot move forward with this new challenge, they must be released.

The second level, that of not being interfered with, must also be challenged to go forward. If that relationship does not provide interference, yet does not give the complete support one needs, one must ask the other: "These are the things that I feel I need in relationship. I would like to have them from you. Are you capable of giving them to me? Do you also desire to meet this goal?" If after much discussion and desire to reach a mutual conclusion, one finds that this relationship is not capable of working toward a mutual goal, one must also relinquish this relationship, as one who is in pursuit of a life's goal must not be interfered with and must receive support. Therefore, one must look at one's relationships to determine whether they are truly supportive.

When one is seeking true relationship, and is not encumbered by a current relationship, one is more free to make choices, to make decisions. This is a most critical point, as the ability to continue toward that life's goal can only be accomplished when one is in right relationship. Therefore, one must be most cautious. One must allow one's self to pursue this relationship only to a point, and if it is not moving in a mutual direction, one must release it. That is why it is most important not to engage in sexual relationship until both have made the commitment to mutual goals. If that relationship is consummated in sexual relationship prior to commitment to mutual goals, there will be much pain at the time that one realizes one must release this relationship, as sexual relationship is most bonding. It is important when finding one's life-mate, that one determine that both are pursuing the same goal or goals before one engages in sexual fulfillment, as this bond will cause much pain and confusion.

If one has restrained oneself, and allowed the separation at the time that it is apparent that one must release the other, there will be more a sense of relief than a sense of pain and confusion. One will then be free to say that we looked to see if we had mutual goals, we realize we do not, and therefore we must part. I will continue to think of you fondly, yet I must go forward and find the true relationship I need to fulfill my purpose.

Thus we can see that love is the mutual pursuit of one's purpose. Choose that person to be in right relationship, so that one is supported toward the fulfillment of one's purpose. When the purpose is mutual, both are supported. It is not that one is supported, but it is a mutual support system. Often one is aware of one's purpose, and the other person is not. As they come into relationship and the purpose is discussed, it will, if the person is ready, ring true. If the person is not ready to move forward to meeting their purpose, there will be resistance and fear, and the person will emotionally protect oneself. This will cause the relationship to become stagnant on that level, though it may proceed on other levels. It may proceed in sexual desire, it may proceed in enjoyment of fun, but it will not be able to proceed at the level of higher purpose.

There are many who share similar goals. These goals are not truly defined. Therefore it is not that there is only one person with whom one can be in true relationship. It is that as those move together who have a common goal, this goal will define itself further into a more distinct higher purpose. Therefore, if one has a sense that one needs to help bring love into the world, one will seek another who desires to bring love into the world. Yet it will be the details of how this is to be accomplished that will become refined as they move together. If one is a teacher and one is a doctor, and both feel they want to serve, it is this common purpose of loving and giving that will cause them to support one another's purpose. There are those who have a highly refined sense of purpose. Their purpose is more specific and is already known to them. They will need to be with one who can be most devoted to that specific purpose. Therefore, there is even more selectivity needed, yet it is the pursuit of mutual goals that is the criteria for relationship.

The media would have one believe that the basis for relationship is sexual attraction, attraction to the physical, and a desire to experience the excitement of what is in the world. Therefore both are always receiving, and both are looking to the other to receive what it is they need. In right relationship, the attraction goes beyond the physical to the attraction of common purpose and the acceptance of one another as they truly are. There may even need to be more time spent finding those things that one can enjoy for fun as the sense of purpose is quickly established. One who loves and chooses to bring forth the fulfillment of specific goals in their life must look to all of their relationships. None of these relationships should be allowed to provide clutter. When one looks at one's relationships, they must determine: "Can I ask for a change within this relationship so that I can continue with what I need to do, or must I allow this relationship to be released?"

One must spend time encountering each relationship and deciding whether it can be pursued or it must be released. One can probe, one can ask questions, one can invite, but at some point one must make a decision. Those people who have made great contributions have done so with the support needed. There are many who had much they could contribute to the world, yet were not able to due to attachments to relationships that were not supportive. Much time, even lifetimes, can be lost in relationships that are destructive, or relationships that are simply not supportive, and neither person is able to move forward into giving that which they are to give to the world. When relationships are not of the right match, not having the right set of attributes of giving support, much energy is spent in simply trying to keep those relationships alive in the midst of this lack of understanding, or even chaos. The energy and time that these relationships require takes one away from working toward one's own goals and sense of purpose. Therefore, it is important when one has a sense of purpose, that one examine all that is within their life to determine if it truly supports that which they believe they are to contribute.

Love supports. Love allows for the growth and development of the other. It provides the space when needed, the support when needed, the loving touch and assistance when needed, and the impetus for growth as it is needed. This impetus for growth can feel like the other is challenging, is perhaps even being unloving, yet this acknowledgement of truth, and the giving of truth to the other, is part of the support that is needed. All the relationships in one's life should be able to provide these forms of support.

A loving relationship will engage your whole mind, your whole being in a wonderful effort toward fulfillment. This engagement will provide the support and strength one needs to feel that sense of accomplishment in the world. It will be a source of joy, a source of mutual respect, and a sense of bonding and completion that cannot be found in relationships that do not have this mutual purpose. It will promote the growth of each individual, it will provide for the nourishment of each individual, and it will assist in the unfolding of the mutual purpose.

Love binds together that which is of mutual purpose. That is why there are those with whom one feels an intrinsic bond though one does not know them personally. When one meets someone and feels instantaneously that there is a bond, a connection, it is because at a deeper level one recognizes a common bond, a common goal. These intrinsic relationships are further nourished by becoming involved more personally in the pursuit of purpose and the enjoyment of mutual pleasures. As these intrinsic relationships are allowed to grow, they provide a source of stability and strength that cause each to flourish.

Love is the source of strength, of nourishment, of bonding, and of joy. It brings people into right contact and provides for mutual growth. This mutual growth brings about the fulfillment of purpose, and the world receives its blessing. Therefore, part of one's purpose is being in right relationship so that one can move forward to bless the world. All the world is blessed by the loving bond that unites the two in relationship.

As you find that which gives you a sense of purpose, consider that the relationships in your life need to support that purpose. Let this purpose prevail. Let yourself be supported by those relationships that strengthen and nourish your purpose, that you might have that experience of love, and that the world might be the recipient of that love.

Love finds fulfillment in expression. When one loves, it is not enough to be filled up. One must be allowed to overflow. This love fills one like a cup that continues to receive beyond its capacity, and once it is filled to capacity, it spills over into the world. Love is directed outward. It flows up to all who would receive. Love fills a vacuum that cannot be filled by any other means. Therefore, if one is not responsive to love that comes to them, they remain a vacuum. This vacuum will continue to desire fulfillment. If it is not filled with love, it will be filled with the glitter of the world. The glitter of the world is the fun, the material objects, the status, the recreational sex, the incomplete relationships that are prolific in society. As one continues to try to fill this vacuum with the glitter, one is continually hungry. It is like one whose diet consists of sugars, of fats, of those things that fill but do not nourish the body. Thus the body is always hungry, always crying out for the nutrition that would cause it to be full of health.

Much of the illness in society is caused by being filled with that which cannot fulfill. As one fills one's body with food that has been robbed of its nutrients, that has additives that are not healthy, that continues to deplete the body, the body desires more and more of that which does not fulfill its needs. Society is filled with those addicted to alcohol, to sugar, to those things which do not fulfill its needs. These addictions are the result of the body's crying out for more of what it needs, and yet being deprived. It is when one confuses the body's real needs with those perceived needs that addiction occurs.

This is also true of the spiritual vacuum. The spiritual vacuum cries for those things that would fulfill. It reaches out for love. When it is filled with those relationships that are unhealthy, with those things of the world that cannot satisfy, it may starve. In its starving, it becomes addicted to the things which cannot fulfill it. Thus society is filled with addictions to money, to sex, to youth, to acquisition, while the true hunger is for love.

Do not think that you can deny that for which your body and your spiritual vacuum have been created. It is like the roots of a plant reaching out for nutrients. It can accept only that which will cause the plant to grow. Therefore, when it does not receive the proper nutrients, the plant begins to wither and die. This is also true of the body and of the spiritual vacuum. If they are denied the nutrients needed for growth, they too begin to wither and die. There is much among the society that is needless. It is a walking death. It has the appearance of life, but if pursued, one can sense the emptiness that truly exists. The body becomes tight, the skin becomes taut, the eyes become hollow, and the lifeforce is not free to move throughout the body. When the spiritual vacuum begins to wither and die, one sees emptiness, one sees shallowness in relationship, one sees lack of purpose, one sees a philosophy that says, "Take it all now, as tomorrow it will all be gone," rather than, "Grow today, that you might become more."

When one is open to receiving that which one needs for the body and the spiritual vacuum, one grows like a strong, healthy plant. One is full of lifeforce, of enthusiasm, of positive desire, and of a feeling of being centered. When one is open to these nutrients, one is most aware of one's environment. One's sensitivity becomes heightened. As one eliminates those foods that are not a positive factor in their growth, one develops a sensitivity toward those foods, and it becomes difficult for them to be tolerated.

As one grows spiritually in Love, one is less able to tolerate the shallowness in relationships, the vindictiveness that one sees in the workplace, and the hatred that one encounters in the world. One is most sensitive to these things, and responds in a way that is disruptive. That is because as one becomes filled with Love, one becomes a most disturbing element in the presence of this hatred, of this vindictiveness, of this shallowness of relationship.

As the body thrives on those nutrients that it needs, the spiritual vacuum thrives on that which is fulfilling. The spiritual vacuum needs true relationship, needs meditation, needs one to be with Love. As one grows in relation to one's Higher Self, one increases in capacity to accept Love. As the capacity for accepting Love grows, one therefore is able to spill that Love into the world and becomes a channel for Love. Therefore, these steps for becoming a channel for Love are to become in tune with one's Higher Self; to open oneself up to Love; and to allow Love to flow through them into the world. This Love is a spiritual life force, an energy that cannot be contained. Therefore, once one has been filled to capacity, one cannot contain the Love that continues to flow through. It has nowhere to go but out into the world. When one has attained the level of being a channel for Love, one cannot return to the spiritual emptiness that one previously experienced without withering and dying spiritually.

Thus Love opens one to the world, and once opened, that person must be most discerning. As one progresses on this spiritual path of life, one will have many new experiences. Each new experience will be both a challenge and an opportunity to allow God's Love into the world. These challenges and opportunities are never faced alone, for the channel for Love is never alone. As the person who is a channel for Love continues to receive Love, Love continues to flow through them. This Love accompanies them into every situation, and profound intuition provides the answers for dealing with these new experiences. Therefore, the channel for Love must be most in tune with one's Higher Self and able to respond.

Love is the ultimate acceptance of one's Source, and this complete acceptance brings one to peace. Thus Love is a journey into oneself, a deepening understanding of all, and an awareness of one's unity with all that is. As one grows in this understanding, one realizes that Love is the force, the magnet, that brings all to that understanding of unity. That unity is the Universe. The Universe encompasses all, and there is no separation. It is only as each person chooses not to be separate that they are brought Home. Therefore your choice to become a channel for Love, to be open to intuition, to be accepting of Love and growing in that capacity, is the initiation into the journey Home.

Love is power. Its power is greater than any other. Once one has been claimed by Love, all other forces are powerless before it. Therefore the channel for Love need not be afraid as Love overcomes all else. This is not to say that the person need not be discerning, for Love is a most disruptive force and one must always be protecting oneself from those who would strike out. Yet, if one follows one's intuition, if one continues to be filled with Love, one will overcome the world.

Jesus was a man who, through Love, overcame the world. His life is an example of the power and the magnitude, the magnetism and the disruption, of the power of Love. When one studies His life, one can see the force of Love in action, yet those who were unable to receive rejected Him. When one is a channel for Love, one will experience much rejection. Yet Love overcomes the world and this rejection must be seen in the light of the total occurrence. As one is rejected for Love, one is at the same time claiming the power of Love. For Love is greater than the experience of rejection. It is the world that is like a child, afraid and vindictive toward all it cannot understand. One would not be angry at a child for being afraid of what he does not understand. Thus one, too, is not to be angry at the world for rejection, for the world is simply rejecting and afraid of what it does not understand.

As the decision to be a channel for Love is made, that commitment causes one to burst out of the stage of being a bud into the stage of blossoming. It is this blossoming that will take one through the experience of fulfilling their purpose, and thus, return Home. The journey Home begins with the commitment to purpose, to being a channel for Love, and to following one's path wherever that path may lead. The journey of the channel for Love is the fulfillment of the spiritual vacuum. As the body accepts healthy nutrients and glows with the radiance of health, so the channel for Love glows with the radiance of the power of Love. It is this radiance to which others will respond. They will respond with acceptance or rejection. Neither is to be condemned nor judged. It is simply a response. Those who reject at this point in history will be those who accept at a future time. Therefore, when you experience rejection, experience it only as the other is not yet ready, and move forward with those who are ready to accept. When one is on the spiritual path, one must be able to release all who are not ready to respond so that one can be in relationship with those who may respond.

The commitment to the spiritual path brings the complete fulfillment of the heart's desire, and none can take away this joy.

Love is the culmination of the journey toward the Source of one's being. Love chooses to follow that which it can only follow. It can follow nothing else. Therefore, when one chooses to live one's life in Love, one is choosing to return to God. Love is the greatest power on earth. It far exceeds notions of romantic love. It unifies all that it touches. In romantic love there is separation, there is great desire for union, and there are moments of union. Yet, the basis for romantic love is the projection of one's desires upon another. Therefore, union occurs only at brief moments when there is deep acceptance, or when there is deep belief that the other fulfills one's desires. The basis for romantic love is belief that the other matches those attributes one has chosen as important. Often in romantic encounters, one sees only those attributes one desires, and one fails to see other attributes that do not match one's required list and that need acceptance. These relationships frequently last for weeks or months until one removes the filter and sees beyond the desired attributes. At this point, one becomes disillusioned and frequently blames the other for being who they were all along. It is simply that one was perceiving the other through a filter.

In love, one sees without filter. One sees one's own strengths, one's own weaknesses, and accepts them. Thus by accepting oneself, one can see the other without a filter, see the strengths and weaknesses, and choose to accept all. It is this total acceptance without judgment that allows the relationship to develop into one of love. The joy of this kind of love far exceeds any experience of romantic love.

Romantic love is full of confusion and disappointment. It is full of a sense of being pulled up and down like a yo-yo. The acceptance and lack of acceptance pattern causes much insecurity, and at some point turns to disillusionment. Marriages that are based on this notion tend either to stay together because of other bonds such as children or business, or accept that this is all there is. Those who feel cheated, who feel that there is more, will choose to leave that marriage, yet in many cases simply find other relationships of romantic love and repeat the cycle. When one can begin to see love differently, and can begin to look at a lover with total acceptance, one can come into true relationship. True relationship is not dependent on romantic love. It is dependent upon complete acceptance of self and of the other, and pursuit of common goals.

The combination of acceptance and common goals provides a solid basis for relationship. One cannot find true relationship by turning to the media for advice. One must go deep within oneself to know what it is their life must be about, and to go through a growth process of becoming self-accepting so that one may lovingly accept others. This process of self-acceptance takes time, and must be done by every individual. Those messages learned from when one was first born are piled high over one's head, and one must review and understand, and eliminate these judgments so that one can see another clearly. As one begins this journey toward seeing oneself without judgment, one immediately begins to open up the world in a way one has never seen it before. This opening up causes one to open to the love experience. As one opens up to the love experience, one then becomes a channel for Love. Thus the beginning of love is the acceptance of oneself.

Romantic love is a path that leads to disillusionment. This inevitable disillusionment results when one finds the other to have areas that they cannot accept. The judgments that render those attributes unacceptable are the same judgments that one has made upon oneself. In many cases, parents and other significant adults also made these judgments during the years of one's growing and developing. Therefore, the process of self-acceptance begins by looking at those judgments that were made when we were young, and determining the reality of those conclusions. One does not need to continue to judge that certain attributes are good and others are bad. One can see each as simply a way of being or reacting; a value, belief, or assumption; and realize that as the two people come together they will begin to meld, to forge new ways of thinking. Thus these attributes do not remain stagnant, and the two are free to choose the highest plane of functioning. When one can perceive the other with acceptance and love, one is therefore able to support the other, and in doing so, support the highest plane of behaving. This is not to say that one fits into relationship and tries to change another. This is a sign of lack of acceptance. Rather, by accepting oneself and another, the two forge new planes of seeing and behaving. Thus love spills forth from the couple and blesses the world.

Do not think that your love relationship is for you alone. It is a source of creative energy, a generating station for love. As love develops and grows, the couple is filled to capacity, and this love overflows into the world. When one loves, one needs true relationship in order for that love to be generated and multiplied and cast forth into the world. Thus love is far greater than the two could ever contain. It cannot be contained, and the positive energy that is emitted attracts other kinds of energy. Thus love unites all who would love, and reunites them with the Source.

God is the Source of all love. God is the love. Love is God. Therefore, when you love, you are God in the world. The world is starving for love. In every place, love is needed. Wealthy and poor alike are starving. It cannot be bought; it can only be accepted. Therefore, love comes through each channel for Love, and Love blesses and saves those who would accept it. True relationship is not limited to man and woman. True relationship is binding and commits one to the other. True relationship is fostered by the commitment first to God, and then to each other. It is important that both understand that the commitment, the devotion, must be first to God. It is in gazing upon one's Source together that one becomes united and the heart's longing is fulfilled.

Devotion must be only for God. It is this shared devotion, this pursuit of common goals and purpose, that form the highest kind of relationship that one can express in the world. One is not limited to only one such relationship, as one may also find that relationship with one's child, one's parent, with one's friend; yet the relationship between man and woman must not be violated. Therefore, commitment of a physical nature must be more sound, and must be forever limited to the partnership. One cannot enter into true relationship lightheartedly. One must enter filled with devotion, desire for the highest form of relationship, and be willing to be totally accepting of oneself and of the other. Thus the romantic highs one has associated with love have no place in true relationship, as one is making a serious commitment of one's life to one's Source, to one's purpose, and to another. The love that results will be far greater, far deeper, far more lasting than that which is romantic. It will not be characterized by the illusion and disillusionment of romantic love where one repeatedly falls in and out of love. It will be characterized by genuine bonding, by commitment to a higher Source, and by the deep desire to resolve differences so that love may continue to flow through.

Love gives of itself through those who would accept. Those who accept, however, must be ready to give up all, to follow. They must become Disciples of that Love. Thus to be in true relationship, one must be a Disciple of Love, of the Source of one's being, and one must be prepared to give up all in support of that love. This does not mean one will give up all, as one needs much to be able to navigate in the world; yet it means that one must be willing to examine and remove anything that is a blockage to that love. As one commits to one's higher purpose, one is then drawn into that arena where one can experience true relationship. One must be willing to move into that arena alone, as it is only by moving alone that one has the possibility of a true relationship. One must be willing to be alone, to trust, and to move forward alone, so that one becomes strong in order to be able to accept and maintain true relationship. Thus the moving forward of love is preparation for true relationship.

The acceptance of the spiritual path is made within oneself. Although others may join in combination, one truly makes this decision alone. It is only when one can make this decision alone that one can go forward and attract to oneself those things that are needed to bring this purpose to fruition. It is the willingness to take this step that propels one into the path of love. Once propelled, one cannot return. Like the internal parts of the bud, once the casing has broken, one enters into another reality from which one cannot return. One is then to bloom, to bring its complete essence to the world, that one can experience complete fulfillment, can bless the world, and continue on the journey Home.

The step toward right relationship is a step in trust that all one's needs will be provided. Let your desire be for God, and all else will be added.

Love brings all who would participate to the Source of their being. Love invites. Love challenges. Love fulfills. Love rewards. It is the nature of Love to transform one toward the fulfillment of their deepest and highest goals. When one encounters an invitation to Love, one must empty oneself of former notions of the meaning of Love. It is essential that one be able to move away from the association of Love with romantic love, and be able to move into the understanding of Love as the fulfillment of the heart's greatest desire. At the core of the heart resides the understanding of true meaning. At the core, one experiences knowing at its deepest level. One may not be able to express this intellectually, may not be able to understand or to verbalize its meaning, yet it is truly known.

The core of one's heart is the deep recognition of all that is, and all that has been. It can be brought forth to conscious understanding by involvement with a person or thing that activates this intuition. This activation begins a process of returning one to one's true self. Therefore, Love invites, Love recognizes, Love activates and returns one to one's Higher Self.

The acknowledgement of one's Higher Self brings one into a level of more conscious preparation for fulfilling one's purpose. One has been in preparation for a very long time, yet this preparation has been done at a more unconscious level. At the moment one's intuition is activated, and one gets in touch with one's Higher Self, one begins a more conscious level understanding of one's purpose. Those who are dedicated to Love, who are consciously following a spiritual path of Love, are brought into contact with those for whom it has become time to have this intuition activated. That is why, when one is on a spiritual path, one often does not understand why one must go in a direction, or must be at a specific place and meet specific people; yet this is all part of the plan. This plan brings people into contact with those who can initiate them into the spiritual path, which will bring them to fulfillment of their purpose, and a return to their Source.

The activation of intuition is the beginning of the conscious invitation to complete one's purpose. One can encounter those who activate their intuition in many different areas, many different activities of life. It may be within their job, within their family, with known friendships, on vacation, at any moment. When that moment occurs, one's life is changed. One can never return to the former life and be the same. One will see differently, and it can be most confusing if one is not brought into an understanding of the meaning of this change. Therefore, when one is on a spiritual path of Love that activates profound intuition in another, one must be most aware that with this activation will come much confusion and, in some cases, a sense of being threatened or afraid. One needs to be ready to provide that care, that understanding, that responsiveness that is needed.

The responsibility to respond to this intuition can only be with the person whose intuition has been activated. This person must look for support from others, but must look inside for direction. This activation puts them in touch with their Higher Self, and intuition moves them to behave, or to respond, in certain ways. At this time there are those who leave relationships, even marriages, who say, "I don't understand why I must do this, but I must." Who look for ways to justify their actions and cannot find adequate reason; who may look to blame others and yet not find a reason to blame. It is a period of much confusion externally; yet internally, one knows that one has encountered a point in life from which there is no returning.

One may experience guilt as one feels that society is judging them. One may encounter judgments and ridicule from those who do not understand, yet one will move forward with new understanding. It is important to connect with others of spiritual understanding who can provide assistance. This community will support the other without judgment. It is important to seek support to care for one's self and to know that one is doing what one must, even though there is no conscious understanding why this is occurring.

When Love invites, it can be a most persistent invitation. Love is the greatest of all magnets. It draws to it those who would respond. When one cannot respond, one goes through much internal confusion and self-doubt. Fear may cause one to strike out or to protect. Yet Love will issue another invitation at another point, and eventually all will respond.

When Love calls, it is important to realize that nothing will remain the same. One's relationships, one's position, one's use of time will all begin to shift away from old perceptions into new ways of service. It is during this period where there is great internal shift that one can be most uncomfortable, one can feel shaky, and one reaches out to those who can provide assistance. As one goes through this period of time of great internal shift, one begins, after much internal exploration, to stabilize. As one stabilizes, one begins to feel more grounded, and more ready to step forward into their purpose. At this point, the things of the past seem less relevant and have begun to fall away. Those things that remain must come into alignment with one's purpose. Therefore, time and resources needed to fulfill one's purpose must be in alignment, and there must be reconsideration of all else. As one goes through this period, one does much releasing. This release can be most uncomfortable for others. Yet once one has made the decision to accept the invitation to Love, one cannot return. As Love fills the vacuum that only Love can fill in each person, the energy, the need for fulfillment, becomes most strong. One desires to step forward into that purpose. That desire for purpose and for fulfillment are all that truly matter. Therefore, everything in one's life is brought into a point of service with one's purpose.

As one begins to stabilize, one can then be more supportive of others whose intuition has been activated, and who can accept the invitation to Love. Thus the circle becomes wider, and as it grows, more people have their intuition activated and receive the opportunity to respond to Love. It is this ever-increasing response to Love, to the fulfillment of one's spiritual purpose, that will return all to their Source. Thus, Love is the circle that never is broken, and always is increasing in size. As it increases in size, it continues to encompass all, and to surround the planet. Love will bring peace to the planet. Yet, peace will not be something that the planet will experience all at once. It will be an increasing response to the activation of intuition and the invitation to Love.

Love moves forward, and touches, and unites. It is the energy that will bring the planet to peace. Yet, its force is most disruptive. For those who are able to accept the invitation to Love, there will be much unity, both within oneself and with others. Yet for those who are unable to accept the invitation, there will be much fear, disruption, and striking out. Those on the spiritual path to Love must be most capable of this understanding, and must be able to be accepting. It is not for one to judge others as to their acceptance, or lack of acceptance, in response to Love. It is for one to offer the invitation and to go forward, gathering all who choose and are able to respond. Thus, positive energy draws positive energy, yet negative energy also draws negative energy; and it is these forces that can be most disruptive and can clash. That is why when Love invites, much destruction is left in the wake of the invitation.

To be on a spiritual path of Love, one must be able to accept that this is the highest will, that this is God in action, and that one must accept the plan if one is to be a part of it. Therefore, it is the returning to the Source, the magnetism of the power of Love, and the repulsion of the negative energy, that is all part of the plan. Yet Love is the greatest force, and Love eventually brings all to Source. Therefore, when one accepts the invitation to Love, one accepts the journey to spiritual fulfillment and to God.

As you receive the invitation to Love, move forward into the circle that it might expand, that it might unite, and that it might bring peace to the world.

Love condenses all that is, and changes that energy into a mighty force. Love integrates, unites, and brings into service all that one has known, all that one is able to do, and creates energy that propels one into the world. As one begins to discover one's purpose, one begins to realize that all one's life experiences, whether good or bad, can be used to further the work of Love. As one begins to move forward and discover each new step, each new piece of the puzzle, one realizes how a part of one's life fits that piece of the puzzle. The purpose for one's life is uncovered in stages. These stages are like pieces of the puzzle. When one completes what one must do in one piece of the puzzle, one begins to uncover another piece. As this new piece is uncovered, one sees how other experiences in one's life are a part of the new puzzle piece. Thus, if one considers the flower, all that has occurred in the growth process within the stem moves forward through the stem to be drawn into the world as part of that purpose.

Those instances in life that were considered tragedy, that were considered a failure, can now be used for good. Thus a tragedy is never truly a tragedy as there is a positive purpose to be gained; and failure is only another life experience that is brought into fulfillment of one's purpose. It is not that tragedy comes into lives in order to form purpose, but that purpose is allowed to be fostered and supported by these life experiences.

Therefore, positive can always come from negative experience or what one perceives to be negative.

One must also realize that what one interprets as tragedy is not in God's Plan a true tragedy. While the loss of a child can feel most devastating to the family and to the friends, that perceived tragedy is an event where the child's purpose for being in the physical world at this time in history is complete. Leaving at a time others would consider most unfortunate creates the opportunity for growth in those who are affected. Therefore, from a Higher Perspective, it is not truly a tragedy. It is the fulfillment of the Plan, as this event propels those affected forward along their own path.

Each person, at any point in their own evolution, has an opportunity to choose how to interpret and respond to a life event. They may become depressed, they may give up, they may become bitter; or they may choose to take the wisdom from that experience and transform it into a contribution to the world. Choosing to interpret a life event in a manner that can bring forth love into the world causes not only one's purpose to be fulfilled, but also continues to bring forth the purpose of the one who left this life on the planet at a time perceived to be premature.

One must be most able to surrender to God to realize that all happens when it is supposed to happen. One does not truly have a choice in this event. While one may promote healthcare, one may provide emergency services, prevention and intervention will not be effective if it is indeed a part of the Plan that one should leave at a preordained time in order to complete a purpose. Thus it is those who remain behind who must be most willing to surrender those they love in order to be a part of the higher plan. Society often perceives this as a great inequity. It perceives that all should be entitled to a lifespan of a specific amount of time, and that those who leave the earthplane sooner than this timespan have indeed been cheated out of the opportunity for more life experience.

It is only when one can begin to see life as a continuum that has many experiences, some on the earthplane and others not, that one can see that one does what one needs to do for a prescribed length of time in order to fulfill that purpose. Therefore, if that purpose is complete, or promotes another's purpose by a certain event, that is what one must surrender to, as this is a part of God's Plan. All are not guaranteed a similar lifespan as all do not have the same purpose. One's purpose goes through much evolution. Therefore, in one lifespan, one may complete that aspect of one's purpose only to complete another aspect of it in another lifetime. That purpose is always ongoing. When one nears completion of one's purpose on the earthplane after many lifetimes, that purpose to brought to consciousness. As it is brought to consciousness, one must make a choice. One must choose either to follow one's purpose, or one will choose not to follow one's purpose at this time. Yet, one must complete one's purpose to return Home.

It is not for those who are on a spiritual path to become saddened or afraid for those who choose not to complete their purpose, as they will complete it at another time. They are choosing to return and to move through these opportunities and choices again. Therefore those on the spiritual path who have made the decision to fulfill their purpose must move forward with those who also choose to fulfill their purpose. Therefore, those who are on that spiritual path must be most committed to their purpose and to one another. There are few on the spiritual path who are at a point of conscious awareness of their purpose, yet they are most essential in moving everyone forward. They move forward those in spiritual families from beyond, and they move forward those who are less evolved but who are gaining new understanding. Thus the intuition of one on the spiritual path activates the intuition of others. Some will respond to that activation. Others will choose to fight inwardly and deny it. Yet all who have been touched have been activated. That is why the activation of intuition is most disturbing. There is great discrepancy. Some will follow; others will react negatively, or in fear, or run away. The person on the spiritual path must be most cautious, as they must be ready to encounter many different reactions. These reactions may be directed toward them personally. Therefore, once one is on the spiritual path, one must forever be most discerning.

When one is on a spiritual path, one begins to realize that one has great understanding that is beyond what is generally known. This can be somewhat frightening, somewhat isolating, and somewhat confusing. It can leave that person on the spiritual path in a position to need to be with intuition in order to know what to say, and how much to say, about that which they know. They have great understanding of the need to fill the vacuum in their hearts with only that which can fill it, their Source. They can see others suffer, and understand the source of suffering. They know that there will continue to be much upheaval in the world. And while they, in their personal self, desire to become part of the world, to deal with the world, they know they must move into their higher self and accept that which is needed for the world's growth and evolution. Therefore, one has bifocal vision. One sees the world as one always did, yet one sees the world from a higher perspective and knows that one must accept and love the world, and use their life to serve the world's needs.

As the world moves forward in its evolution, it will begin to prepare for a great joining. This joining will be with other evolving worlds. There is much change occurring within the earth. People are coming together in ways that before were not even considered. They are living together, they are moving together, they are creating new forms of communication and living that, only a short time ago, could not have even been conceived. This is part of a planetary evolution that will bring about a greater joining in a universal community with other worlds.

The earth is experiencing much evolution. Other planets also are experiencing much evolution. At a point in that spiraling evolution, there will be a time of great joining. At the time of joining of these worlds, there will need to be much understanding of how one comes together with those who are different. Thus, the preparation for this greater joining is the coming together of people of different nationalities, cultures, and backgrounds. As this acceptance is allowed to flourish, one will become ready to move into the next step of the evolution, which is the joining of many worlds.

The person on the spiritual path is most aware that they are viewing the world's evolution from a higher perspective. They are able to recognize the needs in the world, and to serve the world, that it might move forward in its evolution. As people become consciously aware of their purpose, they realize that their purpose is truly to promote this evolution. Therefore, each on the spiritual path is most important toward the evolution of their planet.

The evolution of the planet will bring about much opportunity for joining. It is in joining oneself in self-love, and joining with others of diverse lifestyles, cultures, and background, in joining with one's purpose, and in joining with one's Source, that one becomes ready to join in the larger planetary community. God is One. God is Source. God is Energy. God is Love. God is Peace. God is Intuition. God is All. Therefore, when one unites with another, one unites with God.

Love is the rejoining of one with one's Source. Love brings about the realization of the separation one has created, and therefore allows one to eliminate separation and be one with one's

Source. Love is the rejoining of all to God. Peace is attained when one has become enjoined. Therefore, Peace is the returning of all to God. Intuition, Love, and Peace are the trinity by which God is experienced. Yet, God is One, and all are enjoined to be One with God. When we move from separation to God, we are part of the great energy of God, and we will be part of the magnet that draws others. Thus as each step is taken, all are drawn into unity with the Source.

The Love of God beckons that all might follow. It is like a beacon in the night. It draws one's attention away from those things of the world, and causes one to focus on things from beyond. As one begins to shift one's focus, one finds that this beacon becomes a mighty magnet drawing them toward the Source. The Source is light energy, is Love. As one allows oneself to look toward the beacon, to focus on the light, one is drawn away from the things of the world, and one learns one can only find peace as one is moving toward the light. As one begins to make this step forward to begin to commit to the spiritual path, one must leave much behind. The initial steps can be most painful, as one has many attachments. As each one is released, one is able to pull away and to move forward into the light.

It is in this moving forward that one becomes purified, that one becomes most sanctified, that one becomes most holy in One's sight. It is this sanctification that enables one to move forward with a life dedicated to Love. As one moves into this light, one finds much peace, much fulfillment that one could never find within the world. It is those things of the world that have held them captive for so long, yet have left them empty and searching. As these things are released, the vacuum one has is filled with the Love of God. This vacuum can only be filled by Love. There is no replacement that is fulfilling. Many would try to fill this vacuum with experiences of the world, with relationships, with material goods, yet these do not fill the vacuum that can be filled only by the Love of God.

As one moves forward, one begins to take on other qualities. These qualities can be discerned by many. One is often not aware of these qualities they now possess, yet their presence causes disruption wherever they may go. This is not necessarily a negative disturbance, yet it is something that causes others to become aware that there is something changing within them. It is this internal change that creates the new tension and can be manifested outwardly in ways that are most interruptive. The person on the spiritual path must be aware that they are a channel for Love and that this Love can create much turmoil. As one moves forward, one leaves a trail behind that is most apparent to others. This trail is a trail of those who have been affected. Many will be drawn to this person. Others will be repelled and will not be able to join for some time. Therefore, as the person on the spiritual path moves forward, the effects of this Love can be seen.

One moves forward on the spiritual path, activating the intuition of those with whom they come into contact. This activation is a strong internal shift. Many have been prepared to join this person on the path, yet will be unable as the internal shift will create fear and they will be frightened away. Others will find the Love emanating from the one on the spiritual path to be most fulfilling, and they will desire more as they experience this Love. Therefore, those who come into contact with one on the spiritual path will be drawn toward them, or will be repelled. It is important when one is moving forward into the light, that one note those who are able to follow. They are to be drawn into the fold. They are to be nurtured and cared for and supported as they begin to take that first step following their Source. Therefore, the one on the spiritual path becomes like a link in a chain. As that link moves forward, others join behind and follow.

As you move forward in this commitment, many will be touched, many will be changed, many will turn away. Those who come must be cared for and encouraged to follow. Those who are repelled must be released with love. All will eventually join, as Love is the most powerful source. Yet some will have greater resistance. The one on the spiritual path is a great leader as well as a great follower. One cannot lead without being also a follower. As one follows the guidance they receive, they will bring strength and courage and direction to those who desire assistance. Therefore it is most important for the one on the spiritual path to receive daily guidance that their path might be clear; that they might not lead anyone astray; that they might move the link, and therefore the chain, forward.

As one moves away in perspective, and can see what is occurring, one can see that these lights are drawn together and are being drawn Home. There is much movement to bring this joining. It is occurring in many places within the earthplane and in other worlds. This great joining with the spiritual families will begin a greater joining amongst families until all are joined. This joining is felt in your planet by nationalities coming together, by the barriers breaking down, by the breaking down of social systems, and the joining of languages. It is most essential to assist in this joining as many will be most resistant, and in their resistance is their pain. This suffering will continue until all can join. Therefore, to bring peace into your world, it is essential to bring Love that all might be enjoined.

The love of God is the greatest force. The peace of God is the resolution of resistance. Therefore as one joins, one finds peace. It is those who are on a spiritual path who will bring about peace in your world. It is by being a channel for love and peace that one affects those around them, that one causes both some to follow and some to resist. Yet it is in gathering those who will join that one contributes to peace.

As one joins, the move toward the Source is most strong. It draws, it purifies, it sanctifies. And those who continue to be brought to the Source continue to move outward as channels of peace and love. Therefore, any link affects any other link in the chain. This is how love will multiply in your world. It will grow; it will envelop your planet. But this will take much time. Many must join. Many must become channels for peace and love. Therefore, as the disciples of Love, you must move forward into the world, and you must assist in that joining.

God will be experienced as Intuition, as Love, and as Peace. Yet God is All. God is One, and all are One. It is only by your thoughts of separation that you separate yourself from that one Source. Therefore, as you begin to accept that you are a part of that one Being, of that one Source, and as you allow your love for self and others to emanate into the world, you will assist in bringing peace to all.

Love is the magnet that draws all to its Source. It is like the rays joining the sun. It is like the dew returning. It is like all that has been created returning to the Source of Creation. Allow your love to flow to all. Do not limit its expression. Even as you are discerning, allow love and peace to flow from you. Keep in constant awareness that you are a Disciple of Love, and that is your reason for being on the planet at this time, that you help restore all to God. As the Disciple of Love, you are most valued. The love of God that flows through you can only be restricted by your lack of acceptance. Therefore, accept yourself knowing that God loves you as you are, and allow this love to ever flow forward. Love is the invitation to the feast. Peace will be with you through eternity.

Love resolves all dilemmas and promotes the growth of each individual. It is the resolution of dilemmas that allows one to spring forth into their Purpose. Those who are prepared to move forward into their Purpose are rising out of dilemma. This dilemma may be in a relationship, the expectations of others, what society has taught that is required, or personal fears that must be confronted. Yet, the resolution of the dilemma leads one to Love. As Love draws one toward it, one moves out of that dilemma. It is as though the power of Love is stronger, and the painful transition is the time when one is pulled in both directions. When one is yet being pulled, one has oneself clinging, or being clung to, and being strongly drawn in another direction simultaneously. This is most painful. This conflict that is created must be resolved for one to begin to have any peace.

  The conflict of the dilemma can create much emotional pain and suffering, much physical pain, even illness, until one is clear what it is one must do. When one returns to the relationship, or the situation that they have been holding on to, they are most dissatisfied. While they may feel initially that they have done what was good to do, what society expected them to do, what family expected them to do, they soon become filled with a sense of disillusionment. It does not ring true with them, and they know they have missed an opportunity.

  When the choice is made to go into the direction that is drawing them, and they accept this force of Love, they are first slowly drawn, then propelled into service. This service is their fulfillment. It will bring about a fulfillment that cannot be brought by the old situations. Therefore, now that they are new in the Love of God, and the service of God, they cannot return to the old, as they will no longer belong. It is that once this door has been closed, it is locked. The future is bright with new opportunity for service. Yet, one must not look back. One must take that step with courage and with much faith. The resolution of the dilemma of being drawn away from those situations where one was most entrenched will bring about inner peace. This peace is the result of following Love. Therefore, Love is the invitation that draws one away, and this invitation creates much conflict and disruption.

Once it is clear what one must leave behind, one must take that step into the future most boldly. One must say, "I cannot be here any longer. I need to go and do what it is I have been prepared to do. I will always love you. I will always treasure the memories of our times together, yet I must go." It is this bold step into the future that allows one the opportunity to be free. Freedom is having no choice but to follow Love. Therefore, in choosing to be a Disciple of Love, one is free from all other constraints. That is why one must be willing to walk away from all that is conventional. They must be willing to leave family, to leave friends and home, to go to wherever it is they are needed, to do what it is they have been uniquely designed to do. As one makes this commitment, one realizes one's assignment. This assignment is one's Purpose. Therefore it is the commitment that must be made before one can know what it is that one must do.

The Love of God brings joy that is without comparison. There is no joy like unto that joy. That joy fills, fulfills, and delivers one to that place where all is peace. The one on the spiritual path must be most serious, most intent upon completing their purpose. They must be willing to step forward into the unknown. They must be willing to trust that all that is needed will be provided, and they must be able to not allow the criticism of the world to compromise their purpose. Therefore, one moves forward alone. One does not look back. And one has the faith that they are never alone, and that their needs will be met.

    The Channel for Peace and Love is most beauteous to behold. Their light is pure. Their desire is pure. Their heart is filled only with God. Yet, there are many steps on this path toward that purification. One is always moving forward; one is always becoming purified. Yet one is sanctified when one commits. This commitment is most essential to be made publicly. It is this public commitment that creates the support, the foundation, for one to continue forward. As many are committed, they form a community of Disciples, and these Disciples are then launched into the world. The Disciple of Love will need to experience much travel as there is much sorrow, much pain, much hate where Love is absent. Therefore, one must be willing to go to where Love is needed and bring Love. God moves in the world through people. God does not have hands other than those of His followers. Therefore, it is the hands of the Disciples that create, that support, that nurture, and that supply; that the way may be known, that the Invitation may be offered, and that those who are receptive may join.

    Do not think that this purpose is for oneself alone. This purpose is for the world, for it is the world that benefits. The loving relationships that are established benefit the world, for God emanates from them through Love. All relationships where love abounds allow God to move in the world. Therefore, love becomes the vehicle, the inspiration, the invitation to God. Love chooses those who are ready to follow. Love offers opportunity, yet Love is always moving forward. Therefore, when the opportunity is not taken, that opportunity does not come again for some time. That is why there are many lifetimes; there are many times to respond. As one evolves, one becomes more prepared to be able to accept this call. Therefore, those who are Disciples of Love are called and have responded.

Let your life be a response to the world's need for Love. Let Love fill you, inspire you, direct you, and lead you, that all whom you encounter might be called. As those who are able to respond move forward, more are gathered to God. Therefore, the joining that occurs brings us to the place we know as Home. Home is a distant memory when one is in the world. Home is a yearning for something that one cannot fulfill. It is only in the acceptance of Love, and the receiving of Peace, that Home is experienced.

Allow Love to become manifest, that all might know and receive that which awaits them.

Love is the answer to the difficulties of the world. Love brings together those that would unite in a way that is most profound. This unity is a most joyful union for those who are participating, yet its real benefit is for the world. The world longs for, desires, hungers for, union. That union can only be brought about by the acceptance of Love into one's life. It is this Love that unites one to one's Source and unites one to all who have previously joined. Thus the union of two is in reality the union of many.

When those who are joined continue to grow, this union becomes stronger, more magnetic, more profound. It is like a massive moving of Spirit that begins to envelop the planet. When those who are joined from beyond join with those who accept Love, and thereby return to their Source, this union encompasses your planet in a most profound way. As this union grows, and continues to grow in the future, one becomes aware that there is movement in other parts of the universe. This movement is a greater joining, and is occurring in all worlds.

Love is the magnet that is returning all to God. Love can be experienced in any world and beyond. This experience is like a great returning, a great joining that evolves, develops, and surrounds each being. Yet there is the opportunity for choice, for resistance and denial in every being. Returning to one's Source is a choice. It is a choice to accept an invitation to follow Love.

Love soothes and challenges, molds, and takes apart. This sun beats down, gently sways and profoundly moves all that it engenders. It brings all to both turmoil and peace, as the turmoil must precede the acceptance. Once one accepts this invitation, one then begins a process of continual preparation which is most defined. It requires the one who has accepted the invitation to pare down, to eliminate all that is not in alignment with this new life.

Some will make an initial acceptance but will not be able to move forward. This is most painful as they feel most inadequate, afraid, and in fear of rejection. Yet it is not rejection but lack of readiness that has occurred. They must be nurtured. They must be allowed to know it is acceptable to wait, as in the future there will be another invitation. Yet all who would accept must be encouraged to follow. This path is most difficult, yet the way is most fulfilling. This fulfillment cannot be accomplished in any other manner. So the one who has accepted, has accepted opportunity for complete fulfillment as a step in the journey Home.

There are many who are accepting this Invitation in all worlds. Many more are not yet ready, and must be invited and encouraged to join. Thus, the Message of Love moves forward calling all who would follow, and making Disciples of Love who then, in turn, invite all to follow. This is occurring in all worlds that the universe might return to its One Source.

Do not think that Love is for only the one who accepts, for the two who unite, or for the spiritual community, as Love is for everyone. Once one accepts, one takes on the commitment to prepare oneself so that one can then invite others to join.

Returning to one's Source is one's ultimate goal, yet most are not even aware that this is their goal. The world has many distractions. It has its own rules, its own status, its own hierarchy, its rules for behavior, its own rituals and religions. Yet they are not the path to one's Source. The path to one's Source can only be found through the acceptance of Love.

The Universe is reaching out to all who would accept. The Invitation is given to all. None will be rejected, yet the requirements are great. One must prepare to hear the Invitation. One must prepare for acceptance. One must be continually in preparation to receive the direction one must follow.

As one moves along each step, one is always at risk of not being able to take that next step. One is surrounded by temptation, by those things of the world that are most distracting and provide some relief and gratification. Yet they do not fulfill the true longing in one's heart. It is only after one has become most disillusioned, that one has completed the preparation for the Invitation. Thus the preparation for the Invitation to Love is disillusionment of those things of the world.

The Invitation to Love will not be heard by those who are still distracted. They will become afraid, for at a deeper level, they know. They will become most threatened, and may strike out at the one who invites them to join. Thus, the one on the spiritual path must be continually aware of the disruption which is a result of the Presence they carry, and they must be most prepared to deal with these results.

As one goes forward on the journey, one begins to grow in awareness of the union that is occurring throughout the Universe. It is as if the rays of light from the sun were reversing and returning to the Source. Thus, as one moves into the light, one becomes absorbed into the light, and joins all others. This great reunion is occurring now, and is the beginning of the greater joining of the universe. Thus, Love calls the individual. The individual who responds joins with others who are responding, and that response is part of a universal return to God. As one dedicates one's life to fulfilling one's Purpose, this Purpose serves the world by serving as an Invitation to Love. Though this invitation may manifest in many ways in many circumstances, it is all a part of the Invitation to Love.

Love binds all into the sea of energy that is God. It is this joining of all spirits that increases this power. God is Power. God is Energy. God is Light. God is Spirit. God is Love. God is Peace. God is Source. God is One. Therefore, in joining, all are a part of the Heart of God.

Allow Love to call you, guide you, direct you, enfold you, and bring you to everlasting peace.

Love provides the direction for those who would follow. Love is a wondrous force which attracts and pulls all who would follow toward Home. Home is the eternal peace of God. Home is the goal of all in all worlds. All belong to the Source.

Love is the instrument of peace. Love is the tool by which one can create, one can move forward, one can experience peace. Love is like a difficult path through a beautiful garden. While one is surrounded by the beauty, the joy, the serenity of the garden, one must toil diligently to remain on the narrow path. The path is filled with many twists, many turns, many challenges. It is not that one completes a challenge and one is finished, but that one must continually take the next step. The next step unveils a piece of the Plan. This piece of the Plan is like a tiny piece in a giant puzzle. As one receives the next piece of the puzzle, one gets another view, another perception of the reality of the Plan. Yet the Plan is so large, so universal, that one can never see it all as one is on the path.

The spiritual path requires much faith, much courage, and much determination. It must be one's complete desire. One must desire it above all else. As those things appear along the path which would cause one to stumble, one must be full of commitment to God. One must accept assistance from beyond to be able to take the step that moves one beyond that obstruction. Therefore, one is always climbing. As one takes the next step, one finds new joy, new life, new fulfillment. Yet as that is occurring, one is also preparing the next step. Therefore one is never finished growing; one is never finished moving forward.

Those who choose this path choose it because only it can fulfill them. That is why one must be most disillusioned with the distractions of the world to be able to make this commitment. As one moves forward beyond the distractions, one attains peace and joy that one did not know was possible. Yet one also receives challenges that must be overcome.

One's commitment at this point is most essential, as without commitment, one will go off the path. As Love moves forward, gathering those who would respond, not all will be able to fulfill this commitment. Those who are able must continue. They must not stop, as this would pull them, also, off the path. One must not become overwhelmed with concern for those who are unable to complete this commitment, as they will be given future opportunities to commit. It is not that they are rejected; it is that they are not yet ready, and must continue their preparation. Therefore, let no one take you off the path.

The garden is most wondrous. It is filled with that which the heart most desires. It fills the huge vacuum that resides in all, and can be filled only by God. Therefore, think not that the reward is small, for there is no greater reward.

Love is a most disturbing force. It is not always gentle. It is not always kind. It can be most disruptive and can create much upheaval. The upheaval in the hearts of individuals is reflected in their auras, in their crimes, and in their lack of caring and concern for one another. Therefore, one must not think that when Love invites, there will be peace. There will be much upheaval. Yet those who are able to accept, who are committed to follow, will receive the peace they most desire.

Love is the most powerful force. Love is God-in-action. God is powerful. God is all-consuming. God desires all to return Home. Therefore, the magnetic force that is God is most powerful.

Love divides. It divides those who can accept from those who are not yet ready. This division will cause much upheaval in personal lives, in religions, in cultures, and in your world. Yet, Love will, in the end, draw all Home. It is only a matter of time as to when, in their evolution, each person chooses to join. This joining is most wondrous. It is a joining of those beyond to one another, of those in the world to one another, of those in each world to one another, and of all in all worlds, and beyond. This magnetic force of Love is calling all Home. All are being invited to return to peace. Therefore, the contribution of the one on the spiritual path is to accept the Invitation to Love, to accept the peace in their lives, that they might bring peace into the world.

The person on the spiritual path therefore becomes a Channel for Love and Peace. As they become channels, peace comes into your world. Peace is not the cessation of war; peace is the acceptance of God. Therefore, allow peace to enter, allow peace to flow through you, that your world might come to a total experience of Peace.

Love is the Invitation. It is being offered to all who will follow. Allow Love to draw you into the journey that leads Home.

Love draws one away from the distractions of the world into a sanctuary of peace and service. Love causes one's focus to change, and one's desire for God to increase. As this desire increases, one desires to serve God in the world. This service is most needed by the world at this time, and also as preparation for the joining of all worlds. As one's desire nature unfolds, one feels most at peace. One feels as though one has finally stopped the restless searching that has been with them for so long. This searching has created a sense of unrest, and in some instances, conflict in relationship.

As one begins to step forward into fulfilling their purpose, one feels as though they are beginning a whole new life as they follow another road. This road is full of promise, yet there are many difficulties in navigating. One must be able to navigate strong turns, be able to avoid obstacles, be able to climb steep mountains, be able to stay in control going down steep mountains. The spiritual path is not unlike the challenges of the world, yet the challenges of the world do not bring fulfillment comparable to that of the spiritual path.

As each obstacle is encountered, as each turn is navigated, one comes upon much beauty. This beauty is felt internally. It is a deepening of the commitment, a deepening of the desire nature, a deeper experience of God. As one enters the stillness through meditation, one comes into deeper God experience. This experience is most holy. It is entering one's Higher Self into the God experience. It is not to be feared. It is most peaceful. It is unlike any other experience of peace, for the world's sense of peace is resolution of conflict. Yet this peace experience, for the one on the spiritual path, is the experience of God.

The world cannot offer this experience. Peace is that which is most desired by your planet. It is talked about, yet it is not something that can be accomplished through the world. It must be found through Love. Therefore, by accepting the invitation to follow Love, one accepts the opportunity to experience peace.

When one enters into the silence, one is drawn forward slowly. One does not need to be afraid, as the God experience is most beautiful, most gentle, most powerful, most fulfilling. Once one has tasted this experience, one cannot return to the world's definition of peace, for it is far too inadequate to serve them.

The experience of the peace of God draws one more deeply into the God experience. Yet, the distractions of the world are ever-present. As one enters stillness through meditation, one needs to allow the mind to become quieted. One must choose to stop thinking of the things of the world and, for a time, move away from those things of the world that are most demanding. When one makes this conscious decision to focus, to enter the stillness, one must desire to enter. When one's mind is still racing with thoughts of the world, one cannot enter stillness. Yet, in stillness one finds resolution to conflict, one finds answers to those things of the world, and one finds internal peace. When entering the stillness, one decides to set aside the issues of the world, yet may find it most helpful to pose a question for which one is seeking answer or resolution.

Then, let go of the question and focus on stillness. Allow yourself to enter. As you enter, there will be a sense of emptiness at first, and after some time, a sense of being filled. That sense of fullness may be experienced emotionally and even physically. It is not to be feared, as it is gentle, and loving and fulfilling. As one lets down one's guard, one's barrier to God, one allows oneself experience of the God presence.

This will happen as slowly as each individual needs, so that one does not feel one is becoming overwhelmed. As one moves forward on the spiritual path, one must enter stillness often. For it is in stillness that one is given the strength to go forward, the resolution to desires of the personal self, and the answers to concerns.

The one on the spiritual path must make daily practice their primary focus. Everything else must become secondary. Therefore it is not enough to say, "I will do my spiritual practice if I am not too tired, if I am not going out, if my children don't need me, if my husband doesn't want to watch TV." One must make the decision that spiritual practice is the most essential part of their life. They must set aside regular times in the morning and at night to be able to maintain the focus of spiritual purpose. Therefore, when one is on the spiritual path, one becomes most self-disciplined. It is this self-discipline that allows them to progress.

The Disciple of Love puts God first in their life. It is their desire first to serve God, and secondly to serve family, profession, the world. All of one's life must come into alignment with their service to God. Service to God is done through spiritual practice and fulfilling of spiritual purpose. Therefore, the one on the spiritual path has made the decision to belong to God. Belonging to God means following God as one's higher authority, choosing God over all else, and being most diligent in practice. One will receive assistance from beyond when encountering those situations where one is being asked to put others before God. When one is on the spiritual path, one must learn to overcome the guilt one has learned regarding responsibilities and the world. There will be many times when others will make requests where the one on the spiritual path will have to follow their higher guidance and deny the request. This can be most painful, and if one is not most cautious, they can leave the spiritual path at this point.

One must accept that those who are making requests have other resources from which to draw. One must allow them the opportunity to turn to these other resources. These resources are made available to them, and they are receiving assistance from beyond. Therefore, the one on the spiritual path must let go following this refusal of assistance, knowing that other assistance is available.

Your society has taught people to accept guilt. Guilt is often the way one comes into feeling obligated. When one feels obligations to others, one must look at the source. Is serving this person in this way a part of my spiritual purpose, or am I doing this out of a sense that I must because of former obligations, and to avoid feeling a sense of guilt?

The person on the spiritual path will encounter guilt as they reject these requests for help, yet they must understand that guilt is of the world. It is what the world teaches. Therefore, this is not from God. God does not teach guilt. God promotes desire. That desire is to fill the vacuum in one's heart which can only be filled with God, and this creates desire for service. Therefore, the one on the spiritual path must be most discerning about all requests. They must ask if this request is in alignment with their spiritual purpose. Those things of the world that can take one off the path are often what one has been taught are good things to do. Taking care of others who are capable, putting others first, moving forward with professional commitments, are all things that are considered good in the world, yet can cause one to go off the path. When one enters stillness, one sets aside those requests, those obligations, those commitments. One can ask for guidance, and then enter the stillness, knowing that they will come to resolution.

Love is a fire that consumes all. It makes the recipient its own. The one who responds to Love becomes the child of Love. The child of Love serves gratefully, knowing that their life is in service to the highest order. That order is its Source.

When one is in service to one's Source, one must be able to accept that others will often be unable to accept them. One must be able to assume leadership at a level that allows for non-acceptance by others, yet where one is not dissuaded from what one knows. It is leadership born of Love that will bring the world to peace, yet that leader will not know peace in its traditional sense. That leader will know upheaval, disruption, and the pain and sorrow of personal loss; yet will also know the highest level of unity one can achieve while in the world.

One moves forward as if one's being were in two different planes: the plane of the world is where the service is performed, where the Message is brought forward, where the leadership is assumed, where the support is given and received; yet the higher plane is where one receives guidance and direction. Thus the great leader is also the great follower. As one becomes a Disciple of Love, one must be both a leader and a follower. One must be a leader in that one must realize that they will be surrounded by much upheaval; yet, they must remain firm, remain strong, and grounded to their inner knowing. They must be able to separate themselves from the world to receive guidance, and to be a great follower.

The one who sees with the eye of Love, who sees as if they have bifocals, must be able to see those who are able to accept, and those who are unable. It is as if when one looks through the higher part of the lenses, one sees with Love the Higher Self of the other. Yet when looks through the lower part of the lenses, one sees how that person is manifesting. This manifestation is a result of the personal self, or a result of the Higher Self. The Higher Self will be able to accept the message of Love. The personal self must make a choice. Therefore, if the personal self chooses to accept its Higher Self, its higher intuition, and accept Love, this will be its manifestation. If it is unable to accept, it will be manifested in ways that are most disturbing, and may result in feeling threatened and striking out. Therefore, the one who is a Disciple of Love must continue to be most discerning.

The Disciple of Love must function on both planes. They must be able to function in the world and remain most grounded. Yet they must be able to separate from the world to become filled up, to receive guidance, and strength, and the ability to go back into the world as a leader. One who is a leader must have a highly defined sense of self, must be able to move through the lack of acceptance of others without losing one's own identity. Therefore it is most essential that self-love be cultivated. As self-love is cultivated, one is more able to love others, accept others, accept one's own limitations and the limitations of others, and move forward with their purpose.

Therefore, Disciples of Love must continually care for themselves, must continually reinforce those positive means of personal care, and must believe in their own worth. They must believe that they are worthy as a child of God, that they are a servant of Love, that they are a disciple and a believer. Therefore in order to lead, one must both be a great follower, and be able to take much personal care of oneself.

The leader will always have another leader. That is why they must be a follower. The leader, the Disciple of Love, will have both leadership in the world and beyond. The leadership in the world will be most human, most able to respond on a personal level, yet will need time away to reflect and receive. Therefore, when one has a leader in the world that one is close to, one must be able to allow that leader time to be alone. The Disciple of Love must continue to be strong, must continue to move forward and depend on their own inner strength and resources, and the strength from beyond to move through this period.

The child of God sees wonder all about them. They see the beauty of the world in its colors and its fragrances, in its movements and sounds. They see the beauty of people in their caring and their giving, their love and sharing, and they see the beauty in themselves as they receive from beyond and give that which they have received. Therefore, the Disciple of Love, while able to discern all other manifestations of disruption and disturbance, continues to see beauty all around and within. It is this double vision that allows them to move forward. For if they focused only on the disruption that is created by the presence they carry, they would turn back. Yet they are able to experience the disruption and still see the great beauty all around. Therefore, they are in a position to hold up the beauty of the world for the world to see.

Disciples of Love must be able to see God's beauty manifest both in the earth, and beyond. They see the beauty of assistance. They see the beauty of the hierarchy of levels of movement toward God. They see the beauty of joining. They see the beauty of the Plan for all to join and return Home. In the world they see the beauty of love, caring, giving, sharing, color, sound, movement, light, and they allow this beauty to move them forward. Disciples of Love are able to maintain their sense of leadership because they are able to see, and to assist others to see, that the darkness that much of the world is in is a result of their inability to see the beauty that truly exists. For the others, it is as if their reality, their paradigm, let in very little light. They see limitation, they see disease, they see fear. They see death as a limitation. They are unable to see assistance and light and beauty. Therefore, the call of Love is the call to move into that light that one might see this beauty.

When one has moved into that light, and has begun to enjoy and assimilate this beauty, one must remember that those around them are not able to see, they are not able to hear, the assistance provided. They are not able to see the beauty of joining. They see only that which they fear: the ultimate destruction of their personal self.

The Disciple of Love holds forth that beauty for all to see, holds forth that promise of the world's flowers, as it moves through its preparation, as it bursts its casing, and as it opens and shares its fragrance with the world.

It is this vision that must be presented to the world, that the world might choose to move into the light. Once one is in the light, one forgets the darkness, one moves out of fear and limitation, one fosters health, and growth, and desire for continued movement.

The channel for Love and Peace therefore becomes a Disciple of Love by providing leadership to the world. The Disciple is one who takes the Message, lives the Message, and moves the Message where it can have an opportunity for acceptance or rejection. It is this Disciple, this child of God, who is most blessed, as their life is blessed by receiving and by giving.

As the one on the spiritual path moves forward, becoming first a channel for Love and Peace, and next a Disciple who actively moves the Message of Love into the world both through their life and their Message, they are most holy. Life's treasures are not measured by what they accumulate of the world, but what they receive from beyond and contribute to the world. Therefore, let your treasure be both your gift to yourself, and your gift to the world.

Love is most splendorous. It is the wonder, the magnitude, the depth, the breadth of what is possible within the human experience. There is no other experience that can compare. Love is the world's most powerful force. It can overtake, overrun, and destroy fear, hate, doubt. There is nothing it cannot heal that is of an emotional nature. Love heals emotions so that the physical might also be healed, as the disease of the body is but a manifestation of the distortion of the emotions.

Love's force enters when one becomes open. It cannot enter that which is tightly closed. Therefore those among you who have erected walls to keep out the light of Love live in darkness. Their darkness is most frightening to them. They are like animals that have not seen daylight in a long time. Their vision is distorted. Their perception is limited. They seem only to be on a treadmill that is ever going in circles. This treadmill does not take them forward. It does not bring in new experience. It is not fulfilling. Yet those who choose to live behind these walls feel a safety in knowing the limitations within the darkness. They fear the light. They fear what will happen next. They fear new experience. They fear those who are not behind such walls. Therefore, when they encounter one who is not living behind these walls, they become most threatened.

The denial of that which they most desire, the Love experience, creates feelings of hate, resentment, and defeat. Their perception is therefore that one must take and enjoy all that one can in the moment, for that is all there is. It is a perception of great limitation, and they perceive themselves only as being in a meaningless vacuum. They attach themselves to any stimulating experience, as this momentarily erases the pain of the emptiness within.

When they encounter a being filled with Love, they become most angry at the contrast with their own lives. They throw verbal darts. They challenge serenity. They attempt to overpower. They may verbally discredit. And they move away from that one who is most threatening. If they continue to stay in the presence of Love, they will choose to hide, to avoid, to maintain their own internal existence. This occurs when they are in a position such as that of employment, where they must come into contact with the one who is a channel for Love and Peace. Yet they are simultaneously drawn to that person, for they are beginning to open to the Love experience. This is most frightening. The walls they have erected are most fragile, and can be shattered by Love. Thus, their security is shattered, for their security is based upon a perception of limitation.

Their response to the channel of Love may be most negative, most undermining, and most challenging. At the extreme end of the spectrum, they may become violent and attempt to physically destroy. At the other end of the spectrum, they may deny, they may undermine, and they may avoid the one of Love. They may respond in any combination of methods that lie between these. If, however, their wall has any cracks and begins to crumble, they may feel most vulnerable; and, at the other end of that spectrum, they may follow. Thus the possibilities of one who encounters Love may go from physical violence to total acceptance. The one on the spiritual path who is a channel for Love and Peace, who is a Disciple of Love, must be aware of all the possible responses. They must be most discerning, yet they must not block that Love from coming through.

Love destroys defenses, shatters walls, and draws all who would follow, to it. Yet there are those, who by their own free will, will choose not to follow. They must wait for future opportunities to join, for they are as yet not ready. The one who is a Disciple of Love must gather those who are able to join, must nourish them, and must assist them in being propelled into the world to draw others to their Source.

The splendor of Love is all glorious and magnificent in its beauty. It is the light out of darkness, the fullness of experience, the fulfillment of purpose. In whatever form that purpose may take, it is a part of the trinity of Intuition, Love, and Peace. Therefore, it is the purpose of each to play a role in the returning of all to God. Spiritual Purpose is fulfilling that for which one has been designed. There is no purpose that is unimportant. All are needed. All are designed to return one Home, and to return the world to its Source.

It is not that one should look at another who is fulfilling their purpose and compare, or feel that one purpose has more importance than another. There is no hierarchy of purpose. There is joining. There is shared purpose. There is shared desire for God. There is shared experience. When one is fulfilling one's purpose, one must be in relationship with those who are also fulfilling that purpose. Therefore, the purpose for which one is designed is the role that one plays in bringing together the culmination of the final return Home. Peace is the result of fulfilling that role, that purpose in the world, and bringing others to Peace. One does not bring peace to others; one brings others to Peace. Therefore, the journey of Love brings one to eternal peace.

The journey of Love encompasses other existences, other realities. It is not limited to human experience. It is the journey that one begins with acceptance, and follows through one's ascent into joining. Thus, the rays that return to the Source are the journey of Love. The journey is complete when the Source is the total experience. While one is in the physical world, one can have moments of God experience. One can move into one's Higher Self for brief periods of time. This occurs during meditation. One can also move into a bi-focal position of being in both the Higher and personal Self. At the end of the journey Home is complete God experience.

No one has seen God, yet many have had experience of God presence. It is when that experience of God presence is one's only experience, that one has completely returned Home. That is why one can have experience of Home in the world. One brings that experience to the world, and the world has the experience of Peace. The channel for Love and Peace will have that experience, and that experience will propel them along their journey of Love. There is no other experience in any plane of existence that is as great as the God experience.

The acceptance of Love is the beginning of God experience in the world. Therefore, accepting and drawing all to God is the only true peace in the universe. All worlds are being drawn into that God experience. All are joining.

Allow Love to be the Invitation to the universal experience of Peace.

Chapter Eighteen

Love is the most essential element in the component of life as it is manifested in the world. When one moves beyond this world, they are joined with those of their spiritual families from whom they came, and to whom they return. Yet while one is in the world, one has no recollection of this previous experience.

While one is in the world, one moves freely, one responds to situations, one chooses one's path, and one makes choices based upon one's values. Yet, one does this without remembrance of previous lifetimes, and the experience between lifetimes. Therefore it is Love which is the invitation to return to that Source from whence all life originated.

Love is the invitation to receive one's true calling. One's true calling is to return Home. Thus, Love is the invitation, the response, the acceptance of the journey which leads to eternal peace. When one is in the world, one is capable of experiencing peace, yet one must focus on a return to Peace, as peace is not within the consciousness at all times. When one is in the world one has many challenges, and choices in how these challenges will be resolved. As one makes choices, one is always learning. One learns by the consequences of their actions. Yet there are those who have been unable to move beyond negative consequences, and begin to learn from their experiences. In those instances, there are continued opportunities for learning.

When one is able to move beyond those obstacles, to learn what it is they are to learn, and to move to the next step, one is moving forward in the journey of Love. This journey is comprised of many steps, yet at each level, one receives much assistance in moving through that step. The person moving through life has the opportunity for choice. They can accept or reject that assistance. When they reject the assistance, they have no other support for moving forward. They can become quite stuck in that level of experience. Therefore, it is most advantageous to reach out, to accept that Invitation to Love, that one might receive much assistance and move forward.

One is always receiving assistance in the world, yet this assistance is brought into much deeper reality when one makes a conscious choice to receive it. All the benefits of the Spiritual Family and Teachers from beyond are brought to assist the one on the spiritual path. Therefore, while it may appear there is little assistance within the world, even at times no apparent assistance, there is always much assistance from beyond.

The one on the spiritual path may at times feel most alone as they gaze outwardly in their world for those who would assist, and it is often at these times that they face most difficult challenges. Yet they have the inner resources to propel them beyond anything the world can construe. The great leaders of the world had reliance upon these other resources. These resources are beyond, yet come to them from within. That is why they were able to move forward, to face all that the world could bring upon them, and yet go forward with their plan. They relied upon resources from beyond by looking within.

The person on the spiritual path is never without those inner resources, yet they are always at free will to choose not to rely upon them. When they choose to be self-reliant only, to feel that they do not need other assistance, they become most vulnerable to going off the path. Therefore, spiritual practice, looking within, and depending upon profound intuition, bring one through many obstacles on the journey of Love to the point of return. That point of return is the return Home.

Home is the spiritual Home. This Home is filled with much love and relationship that is beyond what can even be dreamed of while one is still within the world. While one is within the world, one has deep longing for intimacy, for union, for unity. Yet this is the memory of the spiritual Home for which they are truly yearning. One can join with one's spiritual family and one's Teachers while in the world. One can experience that level of intimacy called union when one is in relationship with one's spiritual family, and with one's internal strength. Yet, one will find complete union, complete peace, when one returns Home.

Home can be experienced in the world by those who are able to choose Love, follow their spiritual practice, and be open to the experience of inner knowing. This inner knowing is an experience of the God-seed. It is the return while in the world to one's Source. One's Source is always available. Therefore, Home is available in the world. Peace is available in the world, yet it is only by coming to Peace that one has this experience. One does not bring peace to the world; one brings the world to Peace. Thus the Message of Love is a Message of the return to Peace.

Love joins. It joins all who would respond. It brings unity, union and the beneficence of intimacy to one in a way that is beyond one's greatest fantasy. Yet it is only through much spiritual practice this can be reclaimed. One cannot take short paths to this reclamation. It must be done by moving one step at a time. Therefore, it is in spiritual practice, in following those steps that are revealed to one, that one moves into this most beautiful experience.

Love challenges and supports. It denies and comforts. It gives and takes. It shakes away all that is nonessential, and makes room for the receiving of all that is needed. Therefore, as one experiences the falling away of those things that are no longer needed, one opens oneself to receive all they will need to move forward on the path and to fulfill their specific calling in the world.

Each is led to receive their calling by experiencing their own inner guidance, their own inner reliance upon their Higher Self, and those beyond who assist. It is as they become more reliant and trusting that they are more able to receive and to serve. Therefore, they must be able to be vulnerable, full of faith, able to trust that which they know, yet cannot see. The results they are able to witness give them the courage to continue to move forward in trust. Thus, as one on the spiritual path experiences that they are provided for, they gain the courage to take more risks knowing they will be assisted from beyond.

The person who is a great leader with great inner resources, who is able to lead others in positive directions, is able to rely on these resources from beyond by looking within. They serve as an inspiration to others to be able to move forward, as their lives exhibit courage and faith. They provide assistance by giving witness to that which can occur when one is able to depend on spiritual assistance. Yet it is still the responsibility of each one on the spiritual path to make that choice.

Love is the Invitation, the Journey, the Way. There is nothing that is more powerful, more beautiful, and its magnificence can only be experienced by those who are willing to accept. This acceptance is the first step of the journey Home.

When one chooses to accept Love's invitation, one begins the magnificent journey that leads to the fulfillment of the desire for union. One's heart is fulfilled. All longing ceases. One is one with Peace.

Love is the foundation for all true achievement in the world. Love supports, leads, and guides from beyond. Love is that which brings all that is of Love to fruition. It is this foundation that provides the one on the spiritual path with the strength to move forward, to move through each step, to move through fear, and to receive the joy of fulfillment.

Love brings one to the brink of true commitment to one's Source. This commitment allows one to respond to one's calling in the world. That calling is the role one must fulfill to move forward, and by moving forward, allow all to take the next step. All are coming together now at this point in history. Those in other worlds are taking comparable steps. They are making commitment; they are returning to that Source of all life.

The return to Source is the deepest desire of all lifeforms. These lifeforms are manifesting in those who are human, and those who are beings designed to be able to prosper in other conditions. A simultaneous drawing forth of all lifeforms is occurring. You are a part of this return, yet it is essential to understand that you, individually, have free will to choose not to respond. Not to respond is not to join. Therefore, it is only by responding to the Invitation to Love that one begins the journey which unites all who would follow, and returns them to the Source.

Those who are able to respond will find their lives most full of beauty. They will have inner beauty that radiates into the world. They will become channels for Peace and Love. They will provide the invitation for others to join. Thus it is by joining that one is in a position to offer the Invitation to Love. As one moves forward in this journey, one moves through many challenges and much beauty. Yet even the challenges provide fulfillment, for it is in the accomplishment of the steps that one moves closer to God.

This journey will take one to unknown places, to unknown spaces where much is new, much is curious, and one must be able to follow one's profound intuition. It is this inner guidance that will assist one to move forward on the path. Do not think that the spiritual journey is for the traveler alone. It is for the benefit of all. Therefore, all receive the benefit of those who would respond to the Invitation to Love.

As one moves forward, one realizes that one is becoming worthy of being the sacrifice for God. This is the highest position one can attain, as it is in giving that one receives. Thus the one on the spiritual path who reaches that level of accomplishment, is the one who gives all. One does not ask, "What will I receive? What does the world have for me?" but, "What may I give? What gifts may I contribute to the world?" Thus one's life is a life of contribution or sacrifice.

Sacrifice does not mean that one loses one's life by violence, but rather that one gives all that they have. All that they have includes their strengths, their weaknesses, their joys, their sadness, their knowledge, their role to the world. Therefore, as one becomes God's sacrifice, one receives all that the Universe is.

Think not that you have come to receive the glitter of the world. You have come to contribute your knowledge and your specific gifts. It is in giving these gifts that one realizes fulfillment in the world. Fulfillment is the experience of Home.

There are no short cuts to this attainment. One must be willing to move forward in faith, trusting that one is guided and supported from beyond. Thus Love is the foundation that supports one in one's journey to Peace. Love is the foundation that lifts all who would respond, that they may return, and in returning, find eternal Peace. Thus, Love is the foundation, the invitation, the way, to Peace.

Consider that you are now invited. Consider the opportunity to respond. Consider all that will be yours upon responding. Consider how your life can be a blessing to the world. And if in that consideration, you find yourself drawn, open yourself to Love. Love does not ask; it invites. Love does not plead; it challenges. Love does not fall away; it provides eternal support. Love will bring each who respond, Home. Thus the acceptance of Love is the beginning of the journey Home.

As you move forward in contemplation of the acceptance of the Invitation to Love, allow yourself to be open to that which is within you. Look within and ask, "Am I to follow? Is this for me? Is it time to take this step?" If your answer is positive, step forward with courage, knowing that you will never be alone. Love is stronger than the earth upon which you move. It is stronger than the forces that would pull you away. There is nothing as strong as Love. Therefore it is that foundation of Love of which you can be sure, and it is the only foundation that is certain.

As you deliberate your response, consider that not only you, not only your world, but that all the universe is blessed by your acceptance. Move forward with confidence that you have chosen that which is of God, and you will be eternally blessed.

The Invitation to Love is the greatest opportunity one receives in one's lifetime. Therefore, it is only a matter of moving through one's internal resistance to receive all that is most glorious.

You are invited to join. Let nothing hinder your response. Love will be your constant support. You will never be alone.

Love is the trumpet that calls all to participate. It is the sound of the music of God that entreats all to follow. Love is the leader that moves gracefully to each, gently inviting, lovingly challenging all who would, to respond. Love is the most melodious of sounds, yet it is most intrinsically related and most deeply connected. As it reaches into the one who is receiving the Invitation, it pulls them in a way that is beyond their understanding. The music connects with the vibrations of the soul and there is a resonance that cannot be explained. Once that resonance is experienced, and that God-shaped vacuum begins to receive its song, no other song is as beautiful. All other music pales by comparison. Therefore, one is able to respond and leave behind all other things that once were so important. One can only respond to that deepest calling.

The music of Love fills the heart where all else has been unfulfilling. It soothes, it resonates, it vibrates to the music of the soul. It fills the vacuum, and all else pales by comparison. Thus, when the Message is given to follow, those who receive the Invitation and respond must move away and move forward. It is this Invitation to respond to one's deepest nature, for that nature has been prepared for a specific calling. Once one begins to respond, one is most amazed at how perfect the Plan appears. It is as if their heart's desire has been fulfilled. All that they have deeply longed for now begins to have expression. Therefore, the longing in their heart begins to experience resolution.

When one's calling is known, one finds new devotion, new desire to follow, for Love is the strongest of all magnets. It is stronger than hate. It is stronger than any force that would destroy. As one responds, one experiences the peace of God. The challenges of the world become less frightening. Those things that seemed large, now seem small. The glitter of the world loses its luster, and one's heart becomes most devoted. This devotion makes one a powerful channel for peace and love, as others see the devotion, and know of a higher Source and calling. One never leaves that calling behind; it is always within. Therefore, in the most usual of circumstances, others are being touched by that individual. The God-Presence they carry emits a power and presence. The lack of understanding of the recipient does not negate the power they feel. They are able to realize at a deep level that they are having an experience that is most important, yet they may not yet have the conscious understanding to be able to relate this to their experience. The one who is a channel for Peace and Love continues to move forward, touching all who would respond. Those who can respond know that they have communicated on a level that is beyond their ability to understand. This can begin to translate into conscious understanding. This understanding may not occur for quite some time, and the one who is the channel has already moved beyond; yet the lives they have touched have been changed.

When one is able to respond to Love, the music of life is more beautiful than any they have ever heard. The music surrounds them, uplifts them, and they feel cherished. It is as if God surrounds them with all that is beautiful, even while they are able to see the views of the world that they must address. It is as if they move forward surrounded by a large sphere that protects them, that nourishes them, that surrounds them with light, that all might see their beauty, that all might hear the music, and respond.

Thus Love is a powerful invitation, and the one who chooses not to respond has much internal conflict. They are full of doubt and fear. They question their own capability. Some are not able to respond at this time. The channel must move forward, knowing that God is present with the one who cannot yet respond, and there will be more preparation and assistance from beyond to help them to respond at a later time.

Love causes much division between those who respond, and those who are not yet ready. This response can be most volatile, yet the channel for Love must not look back. They must move forward with confidence knowing that the Presence of God is always with them.

As one responds to the Invitation, one's life comes into alignment with one's calling. One becomes even more beautiful. The focus on Love, on forgiveness, on caring, makes them like a beautiful light in a darkened world. Their light shines, that all might see and respond. The music of their soul activates the music in others. Therefore, Love unites, Love lifts up, Love lights the world, that all might see.

Out of darkness, out of lack of understanding, out of emptiness, out of depths, one moves into the light, the music, the beauty, the Love of God. One's calling is most uniquely suited to one's nature. It is as if one discovered oneself, and finds the discovery most amazing. It is as if a package has been opened, and inside is the most beautiful gift of light; the gift one always desired, yet desired without understanding. For one does not know that one is empty until one is filled. One does not know that one is silent until one resonates. One does not know true beauty until one sees beyond the glitter. It is in the experience that one finds understanding. Therefore, one must step forward in faith, trusting that the harmony they desire will be provided. One will not understand, yet one must be able to step beyond understanding. One must put aside fear, and allow oneself this great experience. Do not think that one sees and then responds. One responds, and then sees. Therefore the Invitation to Love must be received and accepted with faith. For without faith one cannot take the necessary step that begins the process of unfolding.

The Invitation to Love is the challenge to take a step, on the faith that one might see and experience a different world; and that through this experience, one might contribute the gifts they have brought with them so that the world might be blessed.

When you step forward with commitment to Love, your life will begin its transformation. The transformation will bring harmony, light, and peace into your life. Open the door of your heart that the music might resonate, and that you might follow.

Love is the music of the Universe joining all with the Source. As the Universe becomes reunited, Peace will be known by all. The Invitation to Love will result in the reunification with Peace.

Chapter Twenty one

Love is the Source of all beauty, of all that is worthy of God. Love reaches down and touches all that it beholds. It desires to provide that sustenance of the soul that is eternal. Love knows only Love, and therefore, its magnetic power draws only the love it receives. That love it receives is the acceptance of the Invitation to Love. Love is so expansive that it is never completely filled. As it draws more and more to it, it finds that it is capable of holding more than before. Therefore, it will never be complete until all are within the fold.

Love is a giant vacuum that draws all toward fulfillment, yet it draws only those who would choose to be drawn. As this mighty vacuum moves forward, it reaches into all areas that contain those who would respond. Therefore none are left behind who choose to return.

As this giant vacuum moves forward, its reach encompasses all worlds. All worlds are being drawn to return to the Source. The universe is far more vast than man has yet discovered, or that man will be able to ponder until well into the future. Man can only dream of what may be beyond their ability to travel. Yet humans are only babes in the eyes of the Universe. The Universe is magnificent. It contains those beings that are suited to each environment. They are found on the surface. They are found deep within. That is why even your explorations have not revealed that which truly exists, for that which is inherent in each world is only that which is suited to that specific inheritance.

As you begin to ponder what may actually exist, you will feel like you are moving through a science fiction movie. You will be able to proceed, to envision, to hear in ways that are beyond your scientific understanding. That will make it very difficult for many, as they live within a belief of scientific principles which excludes that which We are able to tell you. Therefore, for those whose minds are able to be open to other research such as that which We provide, they will be able to move and to discover that which truly exists. Yet, those who are bound by belief systems based upon rudimentary means of scientific proof or evidence will be limited in their own ability to make scientific judgments. Therefore, the dichotomy which will exist in your world will be between those who can only accept what they are able to prove by their limited knowledge, and those who are able to believe based upon experience. This new spirituality is experience-based, and will not fall within the realm of your scientific understanding. Thus it will be that the great division of the coming generations will be the division between those whose belief systems remain relatively unchallenged, and those who are able to step beyond scientific evidence, and move into experience.

Already the experience of those who have stepped out of their belief system far surpasses that which can be scientifically known. Those who have moved into new realms must be most discerning, as they could be persecuted. Therefore, they must practice their beliefs, yet with discernment. They must draw others into the experience with caution. They must share their experience with the understanding that it can only be to the level that the other is prepared to accept. Yet, as with all new understanding, there will come a time when it is no longer possible to hold back that which one knows. What one believes may limit one. What one knows can never limit one, for it is always evolving. The one on the spiritual path who is open to experience will, almost from the very beginning, be at a level of experience beyond what those who are held within belief systems can accept. Therefore, when one enters the spiritual path, one becomes unburdened, as those who are not ready to move forward must be left behind.

The one on the spiritual path must be brave, must be trusting, must desire understanding beyond anything else. Therefore, the great unburdening which they experience will be to leave behind all that cannot follow. This may include relationships, possessions, security; yet the desire for understanding must be filled.

As the one on the spiritual path moves forward into experience, the experience will continue to nourish them, yet they must follow a curriculum that nourishes them. They must be in the presence of their Source daily to receive this nourishment. If they are not, they are like a young seedling that develops with so much promise, yet withers and dies without proper nourishment. Therefore, once one has made the commitment to the spiritual path, one must continue forward or one's spiritual life, and hence one's entire life, will wither and die. The glitter of the world can never provide the nourishment that the soul seeks. If one returns to the world, one will never experience that same satisfaction. Therefore, the one on the spiritual path must be firm in commitment, must be sure upon making the commitment that God is what they most desire.

Think not that you can make only a partial commitment, as you will not be able to withstand all that you must endure to stay on the path. Therefore, the response to Love, which is commitment, must be made with great desire and faith. The fulfillment of that commitment will bring one to Peace.

The channel for Peace and Love is joined with channels from many worlds, all worlds within the Universe. Thus, the channels for Peace and Love move the rays forward to their Source, and increase the magnetic pull Home. The reclamation of one's understanding is what allows one to accept this spirituality based upon experience. This new spirituality is another step in the evolution of the return of all to God.

Your planet will experience much divergence. Its small wars of a tribal nature will escalate into division over spirituality. Yet, this cannot be avoided. Therefore, those who hear the call must hear the importance of receiving this Message, as the rejection will cause them much internal disturbance. They will see, but they will not understand. They will reject their understanding. They will challenge and will not find answers within their belief system. They will be lost. Therefore the Invitation being extended by Love is to move into spiritual experience.

The commitment one makes to accept this Invitation moves one forward into deep spiritual experience. Therefore, it is important to give serious consideration to the Invitation to Love, as one may move into that experience which brings one to Peace. Love is the Invitation to spiritual experience that goes beyond scientific proof or current religious belief. Therefore, one must move forward, trusting in God that the acceptance of Love is the provision for Peace.

Chapter Twentytwo

Love is the unending joy of knowing one's Source. Love abounds in the presence of God. It is this presence that fills the longing in one's soul. Love cannot be surpassed. It is the music of the universe brought to earth. It is the colors of the rainbow in the rain. It is the reflection of the sun in one's own eyes. Love fills one to capacity and beyond. It lifts one when one is sad. It carries one when one is tired. It blesses one when one is lost, and it cherishes one as it brings one Home.

Love is not glamorous, but strong. Its strength goes beyond the walls of defense that hide the frightened. It goes beyond the safety one knows into the challenges of the unknown. One is never alone when one is with Love. Love raises the lonely, supports the weak, and brings the empty to wholeness. It restores all that is needed to bring one to eternal peace. Love is the most powerful force in the universe, yet Love knows only Love. Therefore, one always can choose to reject Love.

In the emptiness of longing, one reaches out for something that will take away the pain, and that is only alleviated by Love. Therefore, Love fulfills, Love carries, Love cherishes. Love takes all who would respond and makes them Its own. Once one belongs to Love, one is filled when they would be empty, strong when they would be weak, fulfilled when they would be full of desire. Love knows no strangers, as Love draws all Home. One cannot be unworthy of Love, for Love only desires Its own. It is, therefore, only by deeming oneself unworthy that one chooses to reject Love.

Love of self is the foundation for all Love, as it is only by acknowledging our worthiness that one can accept Love. Therefore, one must be able to move out of the pain of unworthiness to accept all that is in store. One must base one's love of self not on accomplishment, not on status in the world, but upon the knowledge that one is born of God, one is eternal, and one is here to learn and to contribute.

Think not that you can earn Love, as you are already worthy. Think not that you will be rejected, for only you can reject. Love cannot reject. Therefore, it is one's response to the Invitation to Love that moves one forward to everlasting Peace.

The joy of Love transcends all happiness that the world can give. The glamour of possessions, of status, of relationships cannot compare. When one is on the spiritual journey, one will find those relationships that will support one's path. Therefore, once one commits to the journey, one will be joined by others on that same path.

This relationship born of mutual commitment and mutual purpose is from beyond. It was established prior to one's earthly existence, and will continue beyond. Therefore, one on the spiritual path recognizes that one is never alone. One is assisted by one's Teachers, one's Family from beyond, and by right relationships established before one entered the earthplane.

All of earthly life is but a journey toward Home. Yet the journey is cluttered by distractions. One may find, at the end of one's earthly journey, that one must return to continue the work they have begun. Thus one may have many lives in many worlds, as one learns the lessons needed to move forward. These lessons are steps that must be taken to move forward on one's path. Much of the preparation is done before one encounters the Invitation to Love. This Invitation represents their next step.

Once one makes the commitment to follow Love, the steps on one's journey become more conscious. One begins to see the steps as a part of spiritual fulfillment. One begins to understand that one has come to the earthplane to learn, and to contribute to the world. Therefore, think not that the world is about glamour. These are only distractions. The world is about being where one can learn and contribute, and move forward in their journey Home.

When one is taking a step, one may face much doubt, fear, and temptation. One must be most committed to be able to move forward. Therefore, one will find much fulfillment as one moves through the step and prepares for the next step. Love will carry you through the journey, yet it is necessary to be most devoted. Once one begins a spiritual path, one's devotion must be to God. That devotion must represent one's highest priority. Therefore, all else must come into alignment with that priority, which is God.

Joy is the product of following Love. It is the heart's fulfillment. It brings one to everlasting Peace. Let all your prayers be that God will make you worthy of this journey, that you may bless the world and be in Peace.

Love is the foundation on which will rest the salvation of your world. Love will provide the basis for all decisions that must be made. All decisions will be based upon one's desire for God that can go beyond tradition, accepted belief systems, and lack of spiritual experience. Those decisions, where one commits to the journey that returns one to one's Source, will be full of acceptance and the lack of judgment that will be essential for the events that are already beginning to occur.

There are those from other worlds who are preparing to enter the earthplane. There have already been occasional visits, yet this is not yet occurring on a regular basis. It will become an experience that will have to be reconciled within your world. Your world must become prepared to accept those who are engaging in bringing together a universal community. This joining of worlds will be the bringing together of beings from many worlds who are reclaiming their understanding, and preparing for a universal order. Thus the new world order, of which your leaders speak, is only the response of one world to the universal joining of worlds.

You are going through great evolution in your planet. You are moving away from a tribal society to a global society comprised of many cultures. These separations between cultures will begin to break down and become integrated. You will have many new races develop that will be the result of combining those of different color, different nationality, different languages, and different lifestyles. As these relationships emerge, the children born to these relationships will integrate the cultures of the respective families, and the separate races as you now know them will eventually cease to exist. This will be occurring, and has already been occurring, for some time. As these cultures become integrated, as people move to other parts of the world, you will become a world that is of one culture. This culture will contain much diversity, yet will gain the understanding and acceptance that is unable to exist where lines are definitively drawn. Therefore, it will be essential that there be much self-love and self-acceptance for this to occur.

As this is occurring, your technology will continue to advance most rapidly. This will put a great strain on relations among people, which has already begun. Your world will continue to expand its communication until it finds that the management of information will no longer be possible. The breakdown will cause much disturbance, and those who have been most reliant on structure will be filled with much fear.

It is important to begin to base your world on Love. Love will be the foundation on which your world can continue to evolve in a positive direction. Yet, those who are consumed by fear will not be able to make this transition.

It is important when one is on the spiritual path to develop compassion, to be without judgment, and to see with the eye of Love. When one has compassion, one empathizes with the conditions of others, and this empathy gives them understanding of what is needed. This understanding is the basis for mutual support. It is the basis for assisting those not only in your proximity, but around your world, in dealing with the crises that will continue to occur. There will be much upheaval. There will be much fervor in the area of food distribution. There will be great concern about the protection of the environment. Yet Love must prevail, as these crises may also be based upon fear, and fear will not be able to provide positive solutions. Therefore, the evolution of your planet must be based upon the foundation of Love.

Love is accepting. It does not judge another. It accepts the limitations, appearances, and definitions of another. One's own definition, which is their value system, must be respected by others. Therefore, there will be many challenges in your world regarding diversity as your world moves into one integrated culture.

As one learns acceptance of oneself, as one moves that acceptance toward others of the same kind, one must also move that acceptance into all areas. One must accept those of different nationalities, cultures, lifestyles, and also of other worlds. The appearance of those from other worlds will be most curious, frightening for some, and communication will be of a different nature. Thus as one learns to communicate with those of other cultures, one must also begin to communicate with those who do not communicate with verbal language such as your people do.

One must study the animal kingdom to recognize there are many methods of communication among animals that are not known to man. When one communicates with an animal, one can find a level of communication that appears to be a response to speech, yet one is really communicating by vibrations. These vibrations are positive, accepting, and of positive feeling; or they may be negative and full of fear and anger. Where there is love, the being will advance, will respond to that positive acceptance. Where there is fear, the being will experience rejection and will move away. Therefore, one's communication with these beings will be of acceptance or of fear.

One must learn to be most accepting, yet most discerning. As one encounters beings and languages of other cultures or other worlds, one must be able to sense the vibrations, be aware of the vibrations they emit, and recognize that there is always communication present. The communication may be positive and inviting; it may be negative and rejecting. It is always present.

As your world evolves, it will be essential that your people accept the Invitation to Love and join others on the spiritual path in order to be able to make this transition into a global and a universal community. Those who cannot yet accept will be unable to participate. They will have to return at a later time after much evolution. Therefore, there will be much upheaval on your planet, and this will result in much disturbance between those who are on the spiritual path, and those who are frightened and attacking. As those on the spiritual path move forward, it will be most essential that each be discerning, as there is always rejection and persecution when two major beliefs collide. The collision can be most violent as each feels committed to defending their position. Therefore, it is essential to see with the eye of Love, to see the Higher Self in each being, and to note how that being is made manifest.

As one looks through this bifocal vision, seeing the being as a part of the God-scene, one must also see how that being has been made manifest in the universe. Thus your planet moves ever forward, taking yet another step in its own evolution. These steps, of moving from a tribal culture, to a global culture, to a universal community, will be the essential steps that bring all who would join to unity.

Let your prayers be that you may be accepting of the Invitation to Love, that you may be worthy of the journey, and that you may manifest as a channel for Love and Peace.

May your journey be the result of your God-desire brought to commitment, and moving into Peace. May the Source of your being be that which draws you into the final union. Do not be afraid, for it is that union you most desire.

Chapter Twentyfour

Love is the Source made manifest. Love is God's presence in your world, and in all worlds. Love is force, action, a magnetic wave drawing all to Itself. Love knows not but Love, yet Love reaches into one's inner being and creates disturbance. Love's mighty force will not allow one to remain complacent. One will be challenged, will be tossed to and fro internally until one makes the choice of whether to accept Love's Invitation.

Love, when it offers the Invitation, is not gentle. Its force interrupts one's life and creates much internal conflict. That conflict must find resolution or one may become ill, begin to act in a different manner, or withdraw. Thus, as the Invitation is given, the channel for Love must be most discerning, as the reaction will be strong.

The invitee will respond by acceptance, by lashing out, by becoming ill, or by withdrawing. Therefore, when the Invitation to Love is extended, the channel must be most cautious. The channel must also be without preference, as preferences may cause disturbance in one's life. If the channel for Love desires that the invitee accept, and this does not occur, the channel may become distraught and go off the spiritual path. Yet the channel may also not discriminate regarding who shall be invited. All are welcome. If the channel is afraid, this fear will become magnified. If the channel has preferences, these, too, will become magnified. Therefore, the channel must be without preference, without fear, and live in the understanding that is available to them.

As Love moves forward, ever touching those who would respond, the response increases. As one makes commitment to Love, one moves forward on one's evolutionary path. One joins all others who are joined, and all move forward. Thus the one who commits to Love causes much joy in all who are joined. The flock of sheep becomes greater, more dense yet more diverse, as all return to the fold. God is the shepherd, the provider, the protector, and the Source of all. God is great, and Its power is manifest in those who are channels for love.

All who would be channels must accept that there is power and a presence within that is beyond their control. They can only see the result of this power. It is as though the channel were a magnetic field, and as they move forward, that magnetic field draws those who would respond to it. Often the channel is not aware of the presence they carry, yet that presence is made manifest to them so that they may not lose that which they know. It is by understanding this presence that is being carried by the channel for Love, that one can respond to the needs of the invitees. Should they choose to withdraw, the channel must be prepared to let go. Should they become ill, the channel must be prepared to respond as needed. Should they become violent, the channel must be prepared to protect oneself. And should they respond, the channel must be ready to move forward with spiritual support.

The channel for Love must be most diligent in their practice as they carry God into the world. They carry Home, and all that they know. They have understanding to guide them; they have assistance from beyond; and they have the fulfillment that comes with bringing Love into the world.

It is essential to be most focused, to remain frequently with one's Teachers, that all might be prepared. The channel for Love must spend much time in meditation that they may continue to receive. As one receives, one is able to give. Therefore, when one does not receive, one becomes depleted of presence. Presence is always available to those who come into its magnetic field. Therefore, the channel must always be aware of the reactions of others.

As the channels in your world increase, so they are increasing in other worlds. Thus the magnetic force that is the Source of all continues to move forward, to increase and to fulfill.

As your planet continues its evolution, it will be going through much change. The force that is Love will accelerate this evolution, which is already increasing in speed due to your technology. The technology that you have come to depend upon will not prevail, and there must be other ways of dealing with information that must be discovered.

Your planet is but an infant in much of its development, yet this development will increase rapidly within the next few years. As this evolution proceeds, so does the Invitation to Love increase. Many will become channels. Many will respond adversely. This will create much disturbance within your planet. This disturbance has already begun.

As you move forward to commit to Love, be firm in your decision, be responsive to the call, and find your place in the return to the Source.

Love will provide the direction needed to move through the evolutionary process. It will be the foundation which supports all who would return. Therefore, let none go uninvited.

𝐿ove is the element that draws all other elements to It. It is a mighty force that pulls all in Its direction that they might join. Love does not enjoin, but invites all to join with It. Therefore, all joining is by choice.

One may choose to join. One may choose to continue with the glitter of the world; yet one is always in charge of one's own choice.

The disruption that will occur in your world will be between those who join, and those who are not yet ready. There will be much dissension; there will be much violence. Yet this evolution cannot be stopped. This evolution is a part of God's Plan for the unification of all worlds. Therefore, one must choose whether to continue with what one already believes, or to step forward and to be open to new understanding through experience.

The experience one will receive will bring them understanding that far surpasses their limited understanding within a belief system. If all belief systems were adequate explanations, they would be in agreement; yet they are full of much disagreement. This disagreement among these systems has created much conflict in your world. There have been wars. There have been persecutions. There have been walls between and among groups. Yet, those who are within belief systems hold firmly in spite of what they know to be true, which is that such different beliefs cannot all be accurate. It is most difficult to step beyond the security of one's belief system and move into experience that is yet unknown.

The one who chooses to move forward into God-experience will have many doubts and concerns, yet will find the experience far surpasses all they could have imagined. They will need to follow each step as it is revealed, to guide them into these experiences. These steps bring one to deeper God-understanding, clarity of direction and decision, safety, security, and understanding. Your people will need to become most disciplined; for they are, at this time, most undisciplined. They treasure their freedom, which is in reality their chaos, and it creates for them much internal conflict. This internal conflict leads to more isolation and away from true relationship. Therefore, one must begin by choosing to follow Love's Invitation to have experience rather than closed belief systems, and to move into that experience one step at a time through disciplined participation.

Love is the Invitation to participate. This participation will bring one to unity with God and all beings. It will fill the emptiness in one's soul that can only be filled by this experience. Therefore, the response to the Invitation to Love is the initiation into experience.

Love draws all toward It. It challenges, unburdens, unites, and moves all forward who would follow. It answers the soul's burning questions: "Why am I here? What am I to do? What is the purpose of my life? Where can I find assistance to resolve these burning questions?" All of these answers begin to come to the one who chooses to respond affirmatively to Love.

Let your heart be open. Let your mind be curious. Let your will be strong that you may be able to respond affirmatively and begin to follow Love. Love has no rewards other than Itself. It fills the empty, brings the lonely to relationship, and quiets one's fears that life has no meaning. Life is full of meaning for those who choose to respond.

The one on the spiritual path who has made the commitment to Experience, to following their understanding, to moving forward with trust, will be most blessed. They will see with new eyes. They will hear with new ears. They will be full to overflowing where once they were empty. Their being will attract others, as Love draws all toward It. They become channels for Love. God's love flows through these channels, ever inviting, and uniting all who would respond. Therefore, those on the spiritual path will be known by the Love that emanates from them, and many will be brought into that Love.

Let your life be a light in the darkness, a channel for Love in a dark and empty world. As your light shines brightly, it renews not only itself, but it brings light to all who will respond. Therefore, darkness is only illuminated by the addition of light. One cannot take away darkness or lack of understanding. One can only bring understanding that it might be accepted or rejected. As the lights burn brightly and generate more light in your world, so this is occurring in all worlds.

Let your light be a beacon to all, that your world might be saved from darkness, and be moved forward into the unification of all worlds.

www.ingramcontent.com/pod-product-compliance
Lightning Source LLC
Chambersburg PA
CBHW060157050426
42446CB00013B/2879